GERALD COATES

PIONEER

Commendations

Without any question, Gerald Coates's contribution to faith and the landscape of Christianity in the UK has been extremely significant. He has brought to us all a warm, intelligent and lively faith that has led many to accept Jesus Christ as Lord. Long may his ministry continue!

Lord Carey
103rd Archbishop of Canterbury 1991–2002

Honest, inspiring – the raw, readable story of a true pioneer. Don't miss it.

Jeff Lucas
Author, speaker, broadcaster

Gerald's influence on British Christianity over the last forty years has been extraordinary. This is an account of a remarkable man, a remarkable ministry and a remarkable God.

Revd Canon J.John
Speaker and broadcaster

Gerald Coates? You either love him or hate him but you can't ignore him! As a close associate and friend for decades, and one who knows him better than most, I can commend his story as one which will challenge you, make you smile, encourage you and help you to find the grace to continue on the journey the Lord has set before you – read and be blessed!

John Noble
Author and father figure of the House Church Movement

Gerard Coates is an extraordinary Christian leader. This perceptive and elegantly written biography by Ralph Turner captures the man, his faith, and his outstanding achievements in the Pioneer churches. With both detailed and broad brush strokes, Gerald is colourfully portrayed as a servant and hero on the great canvas of God's glory.

Jonathan Aitken
Former cabinet minister, author, prison reformer and Christian writer

I have watched Gerald lead with grace and prophetic insight, walk through sometimes challenging situations with a steady focus, and be used of God in remarkable ways. As a pioneer he has sought to blaze a trail of obedience to what the Holy Spirit revealed to him, and in so doing has sometimes 'rocked' the status quo in some circles of the church . . . but then true pioneers always do!

My good friend Ralph Turner, a very able minister in his own right, has done an excellent job of sharing many of Gerald's adventures in God. May you, as I have, be challenged and inspired to take up the mantle of true pioneers and make an impact on our generation for the Kingdom of God.

Jonathan Conrathe
Founder, Mission24

Gerald Coates is an inspiring leader and Christian pioneer. He has played a central role in so many dynamic and visionary projects which have built up the Christian church in this country. He has been very kind and encouraging to me over the years and I have great admiration for him.

Revd Nicky Gumbel
Vicar, Holy Trinity Brompton

Gerald has been a close friend and mentor to me over many years. I will always be grateful that he instilled in me a desire to pursue a radical, alternative expression of the Christian faith. Thanks to him, my quest continues . . .

Noel Richards
Singer/songwriter

Gerald Coates has been one of the most influential leaders within the new churches and far beyond, for many decades, and in many nations. This highly readable and pacy description of his own faith-journey will encourage and inspire you, with huge numbers of stories of personal transformation, vision and challenge to our wider world.

Dr Patrick Dixon
Chairman, Global Change Ltd and founder of international
Christian AIDS agency ACET

Gerald and Anona have been a part of our lives since we met the young postman from Cobham at the first West Watch Leaders' Retreat mentioned in this book. For this outspoken, radical house church leader, starting up in a tiny house in Tartar Road, Cobham to have enjoyed intimate friendship with successive Archbishops of Canterbury will come as a shock to many readers. Read on to be even more surprised!

Peter and Linda Lyne
New church pioneers, New Zealand

I remember meeting Gerald once and telling him that he was a bit of an icon. I'm not sure if he thought I meant it! But I meant it most sincerely because Gerald has devoted himself to ensuring that church mission stays relevant, gospel-focused and dependent on the leading of the Spirit. He continues to punch the darkness. Where others keep quiet, Gerald speaks out. And I love him for that!

Rachel Gardner
Founder, Romance Academy

I have known Gerald and Anona Coates for thirty years. Although Gerald and I are polar opposites in many ways, Louise and I have loved and appreciated them both. This book will delight those who know Gerald and cause those who don't know him to want to know him.

R.T. Kendall
Author, Bible teacher, Minister of Westminster Chapel (1977–2002)

Over the years, the life and ministry of Gerald Coates has not been without its controversy. However, when the history of the twentieth- and early twenty-first-century Church in the UK is written, Gerald will be recognised as making a profoundly significant contribution to the life, shape and culture of the body of Christ. I, along with so many, have been privileged to know him and Anona, not only as colleagues, but also as friends who have both enriched and challenged my life and ministry.

Steve Clifford
General Director, Evangelical Alliance

At two critical junctures in my career, the Lord used Gerald Coates to speak into my life very directly and specifically. These kept me on track with my calling when I couldn't see a way forward. Gerald has a prophetic gift unlike any I have personally witnessed. I've since been blessed to get to know him as a good friend too.

Stuart Hazeldine
Film director, The Shack (to be released autumn 2016)

GERALD COATES
PIONEER

A BIOGRAPHY BY RALPH TURNER

PUBLISHING

20 19 18 17 16 15   7 6 5 4 3 2 1

First published 2015 by Malcolm Down Publishing Ltd.
www.malcolmdown.co.uk

British Library Cataloguing in Publication Data
A catalogue record for this book is available from the British Library.

ISBN 978-1-910786-28-4

*Adm. by Capitol CMG Publishing worldwide excl. UK & Europe, admin
by Integritymusic.com, a division of David C. Cook songs@integritymusic.
com Used by permission.

Cover design by Esther Kotecha
Front cover photograph by Malcolm Pymm
Printed in the UK

Dedication

To Jessica and Abigail, our first grandchildren and, by God's grace, part of the next pioneering generation.

Ralph Turner

Thank You

As always with a task like this, there are so many to thank.

Firstly, thank you to Gerald and Anona for their time, patience, hospitality and red wine. It has been a privilege to share your lives over this short time. And, of course, an immense privilege to be able to write your story.

Grateful thanks to all who agreed to be interviewed, who replied to emails and who spoke on skype calls: Jonathan Aitken, Steve Clifford, Rachel Gardner, Christian Guy, Stuart Hazeldine, R.T. Kendall, Billy Kennedy, Bill Latham, Jeff Lucas, John Noble, Cliff Richard, Noel Richards, Noel Robinson and Paul Williams. Thanks too, to Peter Lyne, Terry Virgo and David Matthew – three pioneers who helped with my original Masters dissertation on the house church movement. Many of their thoughts and insights have found their way into these pages.

Thank you, as always, to my wife Roh, who meticulously read through the text, correcting my clumsy sentences as she went. And grateful thanks to my 'typo team' who read through two versions of the book and corrected numerous errors. If there are any left, I feel sure it's my fault! Thank you team: Ali Parkes, Pauline Stevens and Chris Kelly. Special thanks to Gill Searl for the translation of the German website relating to 'Calling All Nations'.

A shout-out and thanks for the support to KingsGate Leicester, possibly the best church in the world.

And thank you to Malcolm, Sarah, Liz and the team at Malcolm Down Publishing for your support and belief in the project.

Ralph Turner

Books by Gerald

What on Earth is this Kingdom?
Gerald Quotes
Divided We Stand?
He Gives Us Signs
An Intelligent Fire
Kingdom Now!
The Vision
Non-religious Christianity
Sexual Healing

Books by Ralph

Working for God
God-Life
Cheating Death, Living Life – Linda's Story

Contents

Author's Note

Gerald Coates. Born 25 November 1944. Husband. Father. Christian pioneer. Prophet. Networker. Church leader. Passionate worshipper. Provocateur. An amazing life.

Gerald Coates. Aged 17, 12 May 1962. Riding a motorbike. Too fast. Didn't see the debris in the road. Didn't respond in time to the burst tyre and hit the curb. Thrown through the air. Nearly every bone in his body broken. Unconscious. Four hours to live. May not make it.

But he did. And we can be grateful he did. It was that event from Gerald's teenage years that began the journey. Recovering in nine weeks, when nine months had been predicted, Gerald too was grateful. He knew God had saved him. He knew it was for a purpose.

And it's that purpose that is laid out before you now. The well-known quote says: 'History repeats itself. Has to. No one listens.' My hopes and prayers with this book are that readers will listen (well, read anyway) and learn – that as a result of Gerald and others with him, they will understand the foundations their churches are built upon, understand the battles that were won, and understand and move on, move forward to all God has for His Church.

History doesn't have to repeat itself. Gerald's story is one of passion and sacrifice, controversy and unpredictability. He and others went through the learning and the pain so we don't have to. Building on the legacy he and others have laid, today's church can continue to grow, continue to see lives changed and continue to affect the nation and the nations.

Along the journey we will meet some amazing people: some famous, some less known, but all important to the story.

I've interviewed Gerald and Anona extensively for the book, as well as speaking to many friends and colleagues. But it's my book. Hopefully not sycophantic, nor critical. But true.

At the end of his earlier autobiography, published in 1991, Gerald writes, 'What fights, controversies and tests of faith were up ahead were not clear. They will probably warrant another book!'

Well, here we go . . .

Ralph Turner

1

An Ordinary Boy?

Meet Mr and Mrs George Coates of 28 D'Abernon Drive, Stoke D'Abernon, near Cobham, Surrey. They have three children, a dog of dubious pedigree called Rex and a cat called Sooty (no guessing as to its colour!). George has done well for himself, moving down from Middlesbrough whilst serving in the army. He's now Works Manager in an engineering and plastics firm. His wife Evelyn stays at home looking after the three children and tending to the beautiful flowers that always seem to populate the garden. The two of them listen to the *Light Programme* on the radio in the evenings. They don't read much, but when they do, it tends to be the *Daily Mirror* or the *Daily Sketch*. Plus there's an occasional visit to The Plough as a treat.

Roy and Miriam, Gerald's younger siblings, both love football. Roy wants to be an astronaut when he grows up. Miriam's ambitions are more modest – a career in the Civil Service appeals to her.

Then there's the oldest: Gerald.

Gerald hates football and has no desire to be an astronaut. Or to work in the Civil Service for that matter. That sets him apart as different straight away. He's not particularly academic, failing his

11 Plus. Keen to learn though. And creative, like his dad. A good observer of people. A quiet kid; thoughtful. Very thoughtful. You'd often find him in the garden at night looking up at the stars, sensing – knowing – that there must be something more to life than the 1950s day-to-day routines of D'Abernon Drive.

The Bible says God chooses the ordinary, even the foolish, to accomplish His purposes. He may have been thinking of Gerald.

'Ordinary' may well describe Gerald's school years. There is little in his early years that points to the outgoing orator of later years. He sits quietly in class. Stands on his own in the playground too. He's last to be picked for the football matches ('Oh well, we'll have Coates then!'). And he doesn't mix much in the school hall at lunchtime, whilst taking an early dislike to school food, especially lettuce and beetroot. All that the school meals do is highlight the benefit of his mum's excellent cooking!

Not able to get into his local school, he has to take a bus each day to travel the three and a half miles to Fetcham Primary School. By the time he gets there, he's already tired. And not being local to the school limits his friendships – especially as his best friend and neighbour Bryan Price has been sent by the authorities in the other direction to a different school.

These cold mornings waiting for the number 462 bus may well plant a seed of impatience and intolerance with bureaucracy from an early age.

Stargazing also plants a seed. There is a God. There has to be. To Gerald's 8-year-old mind, it is natural to think in this way.

His early awareness of God may have been further promoted by visits to Miss Smith's Sunday school. A devoted teacher, unmarried and passionate about sharing her faith, her early influences on Gerald are plain to see. Not that he was the perfect Sunday school pupil. Announcing to Miss Smith that the class were getting her a Christmas present, she responded in kind by giving generously from what must have been her own meagre resources at the time. Gerald panics. His bold words have not yet been backed up with any action. The class find a large orange; wrap it in tissue paper and cut out a picture from a Christmas card. It is hard for Miss Smith to hide her disappointment.

For Gerald, a lesson learned. Exaggeration can get you into trouble. And as history will show, he doesn't always follow his newly learned advice.

Shoplifting

Exaggeration is one thing, stealing another.

It started simply enough. Mr Weston, the shopkeeper, is doing his usual grumbling act. The newspapers are heavy – all broadsheet-sized in those days – and it is taking him a while to carry them over to their rack. Gerald realises he only has enough money for two of the Liquorice Whirls. The Sherbet Fountain is just in front of him. A penny too much. Well, why not . . . He slips it into his pocket, pays for the liquorice and quickly leaves the shop. Heart beating, he's aware he's done wrong. There's guilt at first. But not for long.

He can't help telling his friends. They are in awe of him. He actually dared to steal from Mr Weston's shop! The story grows and gets exaggerated. And it's not long before the school bully, Peter Carlton, is challenging him.

'Call yourself a shoplifter? Prove it!'

So he does.

He likes the attention he gets as a result. The hero. The gang leader. He even teaches his friends how to shoplift and not get caught.

Gerald becomes proficient at stealing – Rolos are his favourite. It's not just the attention from friends; it's the sensation of doing something wrong that pushes him. Despite his shyness and his natural fears, he finds something that takes him to the edge of his world. He loves the thrill. Something daring, something outside of his modest home and normal family.

The more he succeeds, the more he pushes himself; 11-year-old Gerald is finding thrill seeking addictive.

The move from hero to guilty culprit doesn't take long though. His boasting to his friends about not getting caught doesn't last long. A plainclothes police officer catches Gerald.

'Gerald, is this true?'

His father is standing over him in the lounge, back home. Mum has been sent to the kitchen to manage Roy and Miriam. The detective stands in the corner of the room. Gerald's aunt and uncle happen to be there too. The shame of having them witness his punishment stays with him. Gerald doesn't know where to look, what to say. He's shuffling from one foot to the other, staring at the wall. Anything but meet his dad's eyes.

In some ways it's a relief. He's been caught. He doesn't have to live like that any more. No need to keep up the façade with his friends that he enjoys what he's been doing. The whole thing has got out of control.

There's another reason for the shoplifting. Gerald was born in the war years, and right through the early 1950s there's strict food rationing. When sweets begin to appear in local shops, it's a novelty. Young Gerald has never seen so many before. He's never had the opportunity to taste them. There's an attraction to stealing beyond the immediate thrill. It's not an excuse for what he does, but it certainly is a reason.

He remembers the day he gets caught, of course – his father makes sure of that. Gerald can't sit down for a long time!

It's more than the sore backside though. There's a tussle going on within this young boy. He knows he's done wrong. Mixed with the remorse, there's genuine relief at being caught. He's also aware that he doesn't want to do it. In this 11-year-old boy, there's an awakening of guilt and an awareness of the need to do what's right.

However, doing what's right still isn't always first and foremost in Gerald's mind. As a young teenager, he takes a job at a café on an occasional basis. The owner isn't the most pleasant of people. He is forever telling Gerald to work harder, wash the dishes faster, and to be careful not to let the black and white gingham curtains get too near the water heater in case they catch light.

To Gerald's mind, there is no way that the curtains can ever catch light, unless someone deliberately pushes them into the aperture where the pilot light is.

Why did he do it? Teenage inquisitiveness, to see if they would burn? Deliberate sabotage, not realising the consequences?

Well, burn they do. It takes a lot of water to put out the fire in the kitchen. At least the owner is right after all. The curtains can catch light!

Shyness and Boldness

The bravado of the shoplifting and the odd behaviour in burning the curtains don't exactly point to an exemplary young Gerald. There's not much in Gerald at this time that highlights leadership potential. Nothing that suggests he will ever be seen on a stage, behind a pulpit or holding a microphone. As a young teenager, there's still a natural shyness. He's occasionally bullied at school and generally avoids being the centre of attention. Most of the time, he's happy to go along with whatever his friends suggest, letting them take the lead.

Most of the time.

Occasionally something comes along that overcomes the hesitancy. Unlike shoplifting, there's a legitimate thrill that begins to grip Gerald. Acting.

At his new school, Cobham Secondary School, Gerald takes on the role of Nanki-Poo in Gilbert and Sullivan's *The Mikado* with enthusiasm – and clearly some ability, having been selected by the teachers for the role from a large number of auditions. School drama, reflective perhaps of some of the later dramas in his life!

The quiet kid has found his voice. The adrenaline rush that accompanies this new-found love of acting propels him forward in other areas of school life too. He begins to realise life can be fun, and he is determined to enjoy it! A new boldness begins to takes hold of him.

Gerald eventually rises to the dizzy heights of Assistant Head Boy. In spite of a mediocre set of exam results, he clearly carries something that is recognised by his teachers – an increasing ability to lead, an ability to communicate and, seemingly, despite the initial shyness, an ability to stand out from the crowd. After all, this is a boy, small in stature, someone who hates football, dislikes sport generally and prefers the 'patter song' of the Major-General in *The Pirates of Penzance* (another early success) to the latest pop records.

The early teenage years see Gerald growing in confidence. He naturally wants to stand up for those that are bullied. He genuinely cares for people. And this compassion is met with an increasing passion to make a difference. Not least because just as he enters his teenage years, there's a moment. A moment that means he will never be the same again.

God Encounter

Aside from the influence of Miss Smith, there is little awareness in the younger Gerald's life of the existence of a God who is real and personal. He still stands under the stars at night, wondering about life and creation, but with parents who have no faith there is no witness to anything other than living life in an aspiring middle-class kind of way, linked to occasional appearances at the parish church for weddings, funerals and Christmas.

This is about to change.

Ray is Gerald's cousin. It's 1956 and Ray lives in Cobham. Not far, but for a 12-year-old Gerald, it seems miles away. It is too far to walk, so it is out of reach, and there is little contact with Ray until he unexpectedly calls in one day.

'Gerald,' says Mum, 'Ray has something to suggest to you.' The suggestion is a boys' camp. Ray is part of a local archery club and all the boys are off to a camp at Salisbury.

Gerald appreciates the fact his cousin has thought of him, although if he knew the real reason, he may not have shown such appreciation. British Railways (as it is known at the time) is offering significant travel discounts for parties of seven or more. Ray has a party of six!

Gerald says 'Yes' before he has thought through the consequences. Typical Gerald of course. Leading with the mouth. Two weeks away from home for a 'home boy' is quite a challenge. Add to that the shyness, and he begins to wish he hadn't so readily agreed.

In fact, by the end of week one, he is sure he shouldn't have agreed. It can be lonely in a crowd, and with no one paying much attention to Gerald, he seriously thinks about packing his bags. But he holds on, and week two turns out to be much better.

Some better weather and trips to Salisbury Cathedral and other landmarks banish homesickness. There's archery during the day, and meetings in the evening. Gerald is concerned by the meetings. This is something vaguely familiar. Miss Smith's Sunday school comes to mind, except that the songs are livelier and the talks more grown up. In fact the talks are what get to Gerald. There's a sincerity, a certainty about the speakers, many of them young men little older than Gerald. How can they be so sure about their faith? How can they seem to know this God who cannot be seen?

25

Caught Out

And then he's caught out.

Gerald has been pretending. If you said you had a Christian faith, you were left alone. But if you weren't sure, grown men in khaki shorts pursued you with difficult questions! And Gerald has been pretending.

Mike, his tent leader, sees through it though. 'Gerald, are you a Christian yet?'

'Er. Yes. Oh yes!'

Not to be put off, Mike continues, 'And when exactly did this happen, Gerald?'

'Oh. Erm. Well, it happened at St Mary's Church in Stoke D'Abernon.'

Mike seems satisfied for the moment. But Gerald isn't. He knows it is a lie. But what to think? Could this be real? Is there a God who loves Gerald that much? Is Jesus real? Did He really die for the wrongs Gerald has done? Is it possible to know God and have a personal relationship with Him? These evening talks are hitting home. And big questions are being asked.

There's a lot of turmoil and unhappiness as a result. Gerald hates putting up a front. Hates that he doesn't really know. The boys his own age with a faith seem happier than he is – more self-assured. Strangely, this religion thing doesn't seem to turn them into fanatical Bible-bashers either. No sign of them becoming suddenly holier-than-thou; no halos above their heads; no sudden requirements to dress in a three-piece tweed suit and carry a large black book under their arm. Real faith.

Mr Lodge, the site owner, has two sons. The longer the camp goes on, the more Gerald notices these boys and their living faith. The way they talk, their confidence, their obvious care for the younger boys. To this impressionable 12-year-old, they become his heroes! He looks forward to seeing them; tries to spend time with them. If there is to be an organised hike, Gerald is careful to keep in step with them. When they gather for the evening meetings, he's sure to sit with them. It is the remarkable freshness of their faith that gets to Gerald. This is real. He can see it is. But Gerald isn't admitting his own need for change just yet. More unhappiness.

And more meetings in the big tent. Sitting on the straw bales makes it seem all the more real. This isn't some stuffy church building with candles and pews and stuff. This is just boys on a camp. And it is God. Through Jesus. Changing lives. Changing Gerald's life.

That is it. He knows he needs to change.

'Mike. Er I . . . I want to be a Christian.'

'But I thought you were, Gerald. That's what you said.'

'Well . . . I'm not so sure. I'm not sure I did it right!'

So there, under the stars that Gerald has stared at through his earlier childhood years, he asks the creator God of those stars to change his life. For Jesus to come into his life, to be his Lord and Saviour. The final line of the prayer that Mike and Mr Good (the camp leader) lead him in says, 'From this day forward, please make out of me what you want me to be.' As Gerald prays, there is a sense of God's Holy Spirit already at work, already confirming the change in Gerald's life, and taking him up on the words he prays. God will indeed make of Gerald what He wants him to be.

2

A Miracle Boy

Getting back from the camp means facing up to a new life. A starting out in a new-found faith.

The first shock is Mum and Dad. They pick him up from the station. Gerald dives in with his announcement:

'I have been born again and saved and converted!'

There is puzzlement on his parents' faces.

'That's nice dear,' says Mum. 'There's steak and kidney pie for tea!'

And that is it. No mention is made again of Gerald's triumphant announcement. Life goes back to normal.

But not at all normal. Gerald can't leave it there. If God is real and God has changed his life, there are consequences. Gerald knows that. He has to act on his faith. Wasn't that what Mike had said at camp?

This insecure boy begins to change. Once so keen for attention for the wrong reasons, wanting to take the lead but at the same time being afraid to do so. And now beginning again. More confident. Beginning to lead, to influence, to communicate.

The Gilbert and Sullivan operettas keep young Gerald excited about school. Not so much the lessons though. He wants to learn, but sitting down quietly is hard for him. Too many questions. Too much to discover. He copes with English and art, but hates maths, science and anything practical such as woodwork.

He's out of his shyness well and truly by this time, and is finding it hard to keep quiet. He's trying out his faith as well, of course, and it's his sincerity that draws him to the attention of some of the teachers. This is someone who at one moment is incredibly immature and at the next moment is showing genuine signs of leadership; one instant, infuriating the teachers with pranks and jokes, the next, surprising them with his genuine concern for a pupil who's being bullied. Caring, offering counsel. As a result, he is eventually made Assistant Head Boy.

Studies may still be a struggle, but Gerald is finding his feet. He is aware that there is a God who loves him; more so, a God who has plans for him. Younger school children are attracted to this increasingly confident teenager. Gerald finds he is able to share his faith naturally. And people listen.

It's an up and down faith for Gerald, though. Despite the increased confidence, without encouragement from others Gerald finds it difficult to keep going. There's no help at home, of course. Witnessing him reading the Bible one day, Gerald's mother asks him why he doesn't read 'something decent' like the romantic novels his sister reads!

The Twilight Zone

Gerald is entering what he later calls the 'twilight zone'. That lonely place between the ages of 12 and 18. A time of growing up. Learning. A time of awareness that things are changing. Puberty. A sudden awareness of the opposite sex. The feeling of being unable to talk to anyone about those changes. And the loneliness. The sheer loneliness of growing up without close friends, Christian companions, mentors or leaders.

From gazing at the stars to praying a prayer, Gerald is changing. But it seems such hard work. He feels he shouldn't be thinking the thoughts that persist. The playground talk of girls doesn't help. Nor does the shared copy of *Men Only* magazine. Gerald is wracked with guilt.

His own expectations of his Christian faith are wearing him down. Aware of what he should be doing, he feels he is constantly failing. His ceaseless ability to exaggerate without realising he is doing it. Thoughts in his head that shouldn't be there. Teenage responses to puberty. He feels he should do better, and that his failure means he is no good to God, let alone to anybody else. Where are those brave words of commitment now? 'Make out of me what you want me to be.' Still prayed, but with an increased sense of failure and desperation, rather than with faith.

Depression. It's a description that those who know Gerald from later years would never associate with him. But that's how it feels as Gerald approaches his sixteenth birthday. There is such a battle within him. He knows what he wants to do, but feels unable to achieve it. His personal high standards have been badly compromised by his thoughts.

And more than just his thoughts. He's not a bad-looking young man, and some of the girls in his school year are attracted to him. They make themselves available to him. And he takes advantage of this.

Linda is his first girlfriend. She is not a Christian, and not interested in Gerald's beliefs, and the relationship pulls Gerald further away from his faith.

More compromise, more regret. And genuine depression. Some days feel so dark, it's hard to get out of bed. There's little motivation to go to school, and none to read the Bible. If he's let down God, how can God even want him to read the Bible or pray? Everything seems so bleak. Where is the meaning to life?

Why bother with school? Why bother with anything?

He tries though. He really does. Appointing himself a counsellor at school to any friends who need help, he tries to speak positively of his faith. But most friends don't listen. And the one time he really does seem to help one of the girls, her boyfriend comes along and beats him up for attempting to 'steal' her.

The twilight darkens the day he finds a photograph. His dad spots young Gerald in the glove compartment of the car and shouts for him to get out. Too late. Who is she? Scantily clad. Not Mum though. A mistress? Just a photograph? Surely not just a photograph or Dad wouldn't have shouted so loudly. Maybe this is why Dad never seems to have any money; he's spending it somewhere else. Gerald's not sure what to do. So he does nothing. Of course, Dad doesn't mention it to Gerald. But he keeps his distance. Gerald's relationship with his father has never been close. Now it feels fractured for good.

At a time when he needs a mentor, a friend, someone to help him think through the turmoil in his mind, the guilt, the wrong thoughts, the depression, there's no one. His dad is ignoring him. His schoolteachers seem too remote. And his friends from camp are too far away.

Making Sense

These teenage years seem to be a mix of growing as a Christian and plain hard struggle, moments of faith and moments of doubt. Especially when Gerald doesn't pass his exams. But despite the lack of success, and sometimes the lack of direction and mentoring, Gerald still grows in his faith. He starts reading his Bible again. Some of it begins to makes sense to him. There's some life-changing stuff in there. He's not sure how it all fits together, but as he reads of heroes of the past, there's a desire to be a modern-day hero for God; to march around the walls like Joshua;

to shout and sing like David; to speak of his faith like Paul; and to live . . . like Jesus. But there nearly wasn't a life to live.

Boldness or recklessness? That's what nearly gets him killed. Why he agrees to ride the motorbike, having never been on one before, is anyone's guess. Bravado again? Maybe. Or just not wanting to look a fool? Possibly. But there is no doubting the miracle of recovery.

Miracle Boy

Sometimes our most important moments are shrouded in normal-looking days. There is nothing special about this Saturday morning. For Gerald, school has ended, and after a short time at art college, he's starting his first job. His lack of exam success is not going to stop him. He is going to succeed in life.

The motorbike is a challenge. And Gerald is learning to like challenges. After all, how hard can it be? His friends think he can ride the bike. Gerald may have suggested that he can. Exaggeration is still very much part of life in D'Abernon Drive.

Off he goes. Upright. Starting slowly. Maintaining the image. No helmet of course. A bit too much on the throttle. Too much of a swerve as he rounds the parked car. Into the debris at the edge of the road. The tyre busts. The motorbike approaches the curb. What was it, maybe twenty miles an hour? Perhaps twenty-five. But fast enough to cause a lot of damage.

Gerald's world slows down. In that instant he has time to regret his decision. Even time to think he may not be looking so cool after all.

And that's it. The bike hits the curb. It throws Gerald high over the handlebars. Still flying, he hits a concrete pillar. Head first. Multiple fractures. Unconscious.

And then God's hand in it all. It's a miracle. The specialist says so. Even Gerald's unbelieving parents comment on it. The initial prognosis is just four hours . . . four hours to live.

'He will never regain consciousness, Mrs Coates. You'd best say your goodbyes. Your son will not survive the night.'

Five hours later, he's still alive. Six. Seven. Seven days. Seven weeks. The miracle continues.

Unconscious for the first week, he comes round to find he is in the same ward as Stirling Moss, the racing driver, who was in an accident on the same day.

Gerald is transferred to a specialist brain unit in another hospital; it's difficult to see how much damage has been done. The initial operation on the brain and a lumbar puncture are followed by electric shock treatment to determine the extent of the inevitable brain damage.

He's got a scar like no other – a deep dent in his skull. But that's it. Nothing else. No brain damage. A number of doctors and nurses start to call it a miracle.

The motorbike accident is a miracle in more ways than one. Not only does Gerald recover at a miraculous rate but the ambulance drivers confide that within a minute of picking up on Gerald's emergency, they received another emergency call. The drivers explain that if the calls had come in the other way around and they had answered the other call first, it is likely Gerald would have died before reaching the hospital.

As this is written, Gerald is alive and well, now in his seventies and without any long-term effect to his health from the accident, despite the fact his skull was split open. Miracle boy.

Pursued and Protected

The motorcycle accident isn't the only time Gerald comes near to death as a child. A little geeky, accident-prone and averse to any sporting activities, he should have known better than to try and cross a partly submerged bridge over a stream. Gerald is carried downstream and dragged into a five-foot-wide drain. His cries for help are heard by a passing shopper who manages to drag him clear.

Then there is Gerald's best friend Bryan Price. A hero.

Gerald is on a boys' camp. Someone shoves him into the deep end of the swimming pool, not realising he can't swim. Pushing himself to the top, Gerald gasps for air before sinking again. Bryan sees what's happening. Diving in, he drags Gerald out, semi-conscious by now. God seems to have plans for this accident-prone boy.

By the time of the motorbike accident, Gerald has a Christian faith. But there's something about a miracle, especially when it's your own life that has been saved, that speaks deeply to you. There's a new resolve. Gerald knows that from now on he needs to pursue this God that has so obviously pursued him – and protected him. A life of adventure awaits. Gerald always knew it did. It's just that this is a different kind of adventure from most.

3
HAND IN HAND

Never one to settle for second best, Gerald is passionate about his re-fired faith.

There's an immaturity about his faith at 17, of course. He wants to be great. He is seeking popularity and fame as much as he understands his newly sharpened faith. But he feels different. He always has been a bit different. His dislike for football and sports generally has seen to that.

There's a new awareness, though, of being different. Of being called by God to be different. As he enters his later teenage years, the desire for fame and pleasing others begins to be replaced by a desire for God and pleasing Christ. He doesn't want to compromise, and there is a willingness to be a fool for Christ if that's what it takes.

'From this day forward, please make out of me what you want me to be.' The last line of his salvation prayer stays with him. How can he ensure that God can make the most of his life? Surely it must involve church-going? But what brand? And where?

One thing is for sure – it isn't going to be St Mary's. Long past Sunday school days, the Bible class for older children and youth is in a different building and in another location. None of Gerald's friends will go with him, so Gerald doesn't go either.

There is no pressure to attend church from anyone else. Gerald's parents seemed mildly amused by his faith and opposed to him taking it more seriously. Gerald's friends certainly aren't interested.

But Gerald's not done just yet. He's an enterprising young man, and he's heard of a Christian youth group.

Friday Club

A two-mile bus journey to Cobham, then a long walk. It's Friday night and Gerald's been brave enough to pitch up on his own. There's a good welcome for him, though.

Mr Jeffries, inevitably nicknamed 'the Judge', is a little eccentric, but he leads a good youth group. Friday nights are times filled with table games, drinks and biscuits to follow, and then a talk. It is the nearest Gerald gets to church for quite a while. And it keeps his Christian faith alive. Though only just.

Gerald's initial enthusiasm is beginning to wane.

Friday Club proves not to be enough. There's only so many times you can sing 'Go Tell It on the Mountain' and remain interested. Gerald's attendance drops. He seems to be falling back into his old ways again. A combination of girls and cigarettes are beginning to take over. Neither proves satisfying of course. Both leave Gerald with that often-felt sense of guilt and failure. The latter is dropped pretty quickly. The former is about to take a different shape. In fact, as far as Gerald is concerned, a very attractive shape!

Anona

Gerald leaves school with a solitary CSE in English. He finds a job with H.L. Reid & Co., a large department store over four floors in downtown Epsom. The store sells pretty much everything, but Gerald finds himself working with the displays and window presentations. It is a job well-suited to his creative skills and he excels, becoming one of the youngest display managers within the industry.

Not that this promotion makes him too serious a young man. Known for his jokes and pranks, Gerald is not above standing in the shop window pretending to be a mannequin until some poor shopper looks his way and he jumps at them. On one occasion, he and some of his colleagues encase the Carpet Manager inside one of his own carpets, with the result that the General Manager is unable to find him!

A confident young man is clearly growing in ability and in business sense. He's enjoying life. He dresses well, with some flair. A uniform at work, but when he's out and about it's narrow lapelled jackets, winkle-pickers and a quiff – he's not going to be ignored! He's not exactly sure what lies ahead, but is aware that the God who saved his life is very much interested in him. The God to whom he said, 'Make of me what you will' is about to bring about another change.

'Hey Gerry, guess what?'

It's the two girls from the Fashion department, giggling as usual. Gerald has been called Gerry from the start of his career at H.L. Reid. It is a name that won't stick though, reverting to Gerald, the name his parents gave him, in every other sphere.

'Hi girls. What?' He plays along.

'Anona fancies you.'

'Does she now?' He smiles and walks away with his mug of tea. Gerald is flattered. He's noticed Anona before; he spoke to her on her first day at the store. She is a beautiful girl, with large-framed glasses, very much in the modern style, which cover eyes that sparkle and a smile that is so attractively gentle it causes Gerald to freeze as he tries to speak to her. A church-goer too, he thinks. Or at least she attended church as a kid. But is she a Christian? It doesn't necessarily follow just because she's been to church. This is important.

Well, maybe just one date . . . Gerald invites her out. He takes her to a West End theatre in London to see *The Sound of Music*. Gerald reckons it's a safe thing to see with its Christian principles. There's no doubt about it, Gerald is smitten.

And so is Anona. She's noticed him from that first meeting – an outgoing, friendly young man who made sure she had friends to sit with on her first day at work. If she is honest, she fancied Gerald's boss, but he's not paid any attention to her. For a while, Anona invents a boyfriend – she calls him Colin – as it helps her to fit in with her other work colleagues, most of whom are dating. But it becomes too complicated a front to keep up, so she 'breaks up with Colin' and pursues a real person in the shape of Gerald! Gerald finds himself thinking of Anona most of the time. He can't sleep at night. And when he's at work, he's planning excuses to call in on the Ladies' Fashion department where she works. He knows this is different to earlier relationships. He begins to ask God for help. He so longs for this to be 'it', but isn't sure of Anona's faith. And this is a major issue for Gerald.

Tent Crusade

Despite the church-going, Anona views herself as an atheist at this time. But she is attracted to the sincerity of Gerald's faith and it is this attraction that causes her to agree to go to a tent crusade meeting led by a Mr Jim Smyth.

Anona is not sure what to expect. The tent is on the recreation ground at Cobham. It feels a bit strange. The only church meetings Anona has been to have been in grand old buildings with spires, certainly not in an old white marquee in the middle of a field.

People begin to file in for the meeting. Quite a mix. Anona is pleased to see there are others of a similar age. A lot of older people too. Some carrying what she assumes are Bibles. Some men dressed in suits and ties. Slightly incongruous with the surroundings!

She's just glad to be with Gerald and doesn't pay much attention to the hymn singing or the preaching at first. But as the talk goes on, something begins to happen. Anona is listening. Listening attentively. Is this real? Is there a God who loves her? Did Jesus die for her? How serious this challenge seems to be.

Jim is in full flow: 'To lose one's wealth is sad indeed. To lose one's health is more. To lose one's soul is such a loss that no man can restore!'

One warm summer night, in the middle of Cobham recreation ground, with Gerald on one side and Jim Smyth on the other, Anona prays a prayer. It is a prayer of commitment to a Christ who is real, to a God who loves her, to a Father who holds her close in a way her father never did. He is a healing God, a God who takes her out of her shame and guilt from the abuse her own father has perpetrated. A life-changing God who gives her a hope and a future . . . and a husband.

And for Gerald that night – he's suddenly certain of his future. Sure of his companion. Aware that God has brought about a major miracle – that God has a plan for him that He is bringing about right at that moment. Not for the first time, Gerald doesn't sleep, but for all the right reasons. He's unable to stop smiling; unable to stop praying, thanking God over and over again for the miracle of Anona's faith. And then fervently praying for their future. Surely this is it? Surely she is the one?

'Please God! I pray you will help me not to mess this up. I want all that You have for me. But, please Lord, can that be with Anona by my side?'

Church Hunting

Dating Anona is a significant change for Gerald, and not just in the sense of falling in love. Anona gives Gerald more confidence. There is more of an awareness of God working in his life. He finds it easier to read the Bible and pray. Everything feels brighter, sharper. Love for Anona and love for Christ bring about a Gerald even more on fire in his faith.

For a while Gerald has been considering applying for other jobs in the retail industry, furthering his burgeoning career in sales and shop display. But with Anona's arrival and the thrill of her own newly found faith, Gerald begins to realise that there must be something more. He's grateful for the job and treats it as God's provision. But to be doing this for the rest of his life? No! There's a different call in Gerald's ear. He senses God has more for him. But at this stage, he has no idea as to how this will turn out. Anona regularly stays the weekend at Gerald's house and gets to know his parents well. She enjoys the feel of a stable family. All is not well at her own home and there is no way she can invite Gerald around. For Anona, it's a time of growing in her new-found faith at the same time as enjoying a kind of family life she didn't know existed.

Very much an 'item' now, Gerald and Anona know they need to be based at a church and they begin to pray together that God will reveal to them what to do.

It is a tough time to be a Christian. It is very much a time of increased liberation: the early 1960s celebrates the arrival of modern pop music, the birth control pill and a sense of freedom from rules and regulations. And 'church' is seen as being full of rules and regulations.

It is also a time of exploration and science. Television is only now becoming commonplace in the home. And on it can be seen some of the first spaceships taking man into orbit. The vastness of space and the challenge to the way people have been living and thinking go hand in hand.

As Gerald and Anona go hand in hand, it is into this new world – a challenging world. One that announces 'if it feels good, do it' and that 'God is dead'. Or at the very least, God is marginalised in most people's lives.

Yes, it's a tough time to be a Christian. Not that this is a concern to Gerald. He's increasingly aware that God has a call upon his life. He just needs to find out what that call is!

4

'Church Isn't What I think It Should Be'

When Mr Jeffries moves on, it is Gerald and his best friend Bryan Price who help another young man to take on the leadership of the Friday Club. This, combined with Gerald's ongoing help at the summer boys' camp, becomes a key component in Gerald's leadership learning process. But he knows it isn't really church, and a church needs to be found.

The Gospel Hall

Not knowing where to start, Gerald and Bryan turn up at the Gospel Hall that Mr Jeffries has previously attended.

As they stand outside the rather ordinary-looking red brick building, they're not sure whether to go in or not. In the end, they walk through the doors, to be welcomed by an elderly gentleman with a hearty handshake that squeezes the life out of them! They are shown through into a large room with modern wooden chairs arranged in rows that face each other, forming a square. There's a large space in the middle, which has a table with a white cloth on it. On the table is a loaf of what looks like home-made bread, and a silver goblet filled with what seems to be red wine. Gerald and Bryan sit on the back row on one of the sides, and wait for whatever happens next.

What happens is a surprise to them. There's no sign of anyone in funny clothes and back-to-front collars. In fact, there is no sign of anyone leading the meeting. A man in a suit stands to welcome everyone and announces a hymn. It's sung without any instruments. Later, other men stand and share readings from the Bible, all from the old King James Version which Gerald and Bryan struggle to follow.

Part way through the meeting, two men move forward and tear up the bread. They pray a prayer and distribute the bread around the congregation. Gerald and Bryan, keeping their eyes open, copy what everyone else is doing. An older lady sits in front of them. She has a rather large pink hat on, complete with what looks like crystallised fruit on top. Gerald is distracted, trying to count the number of cherries. One of the men in suits passes the bread to Gerald and Bryan with a hint of a smile. The newcomers take a chunk each and pass the broken loaf on to the next person. First part of their initiation over! There's silence as everyone eats a piece of bread together. Then a similar procedure for the wine goblet, which is passed around. Gerald is disappointed with what turns out to be a rather weak grape juice instead of wine.

A close-knit Brethren assembly of around forty members, mainly middle-aged and older, they welcome the two newcomers. It isn't long before Anona joins as well and for the next six years this style of church becomes home for them.

A youth group is formed. Gerald, Anona and Bryan are natural evangelists. Young people are attracted to them. There's a confidence about the three of them and they can often be found in the town centre preaching the gospel. With some success too. The youth group begins to grow, with new converts to the Christian faith.

Youth meetings are typically on a Friday evening. Gerald is trusted with one of the keys to the hall, and they meet in the back room – a little cosier than the main one. Often they start their evenings with games – indoors in winter, over at the park in the summer – and then Gerald shares from the Bible. He's getting quite good at this: taking passages and applying it to the lives of the youngsters in front of him. He uses the Revised Standard Version of the Bible, which is frowned upon by the elders of the church, who tend to insist on the King James Version for reasons Gerald can't fathom, but put up with as the elders can see the significant effect that Gerald, Anona and Bryan are having on young lives.

The seasons pass in a tumble of street evangelism, Friday night meetings and other activities. There is a pattern to the adult meetings, held at the Gospel Hall, as well. Sunday morning meetings 'around the table', as the Lord's Supper is celebrated. Sunday evenings at 6.30 till 7.30 precisely for the gospel preach. Midweek Bible studies and prayer meetings. And visiting speakers.

A missionary from Portugal makes a significant impression on Gerald, particularly when, at the end of the meeting, he comes over and says to Gerald 'God is going to use you in a very special way, young man – I just know it.' It's the first time Gerald has received a prophetic word from someone. It isn't going to be the last.

Water Baptism

It is during the early days at the Gospel Hall that Gerald first hears of baptism in water. It's not something he remembers being mentioned before. But if that's what the Bible says, that's what Gerald wants! A Mr Amess, one of the elders, takes him through the preliminaries.

'Why do you want to be baptised, Gerald?'

'Because it's what the Bible says! I want all that God has for me.'

The passion is there alright. Not yet honed in terms of a ministry or serving in any particular capacity, but Mr Amess can see the raw faith that night.

The baptistry itself is cleverly hidden under the floorboards. Just big enough for Gerald, at one evening meeting, to be lowered into about four feet of warm water and totally immersed. Remembering to hold his breath, Gerald allows Mr Amess to bring him back up out of the water to polite applause from the congregation.

'Yes!' shouts Gerald, 'Yes!'

Not a typically Brethren response, but the congregation that night continue to smile and applaud. Gerald's heart is pumping. He knows God loves him. The doubts are gone. Jesus really is who he says he is. He still changes lives. He's changed Gerald's and everyone is going to know about it!

Gerald has the card still. There's a quote from Isaiah and the words written by Mr Amess: 'The Lord's day, July 25th, 1965.'

For nearly three years, Gerald, Anona and Bryan work with the Brethren assembly. They are joined by Jennifer, Bryan's girlfriend, and together keep the hall looking spotless, put the chairs out, lead the youth group, preach on the streets and much more.

It is some of the 'much more' that bothers Anona. She and her girlfriends are asked not to wear make-up. The youth are encouraged not to drink or smoke. The cinema is frowned upon too. And no television on Sundays. None of these things really bother the youngsters. But not being able to speak in the meetings is a problem. For the girls, that is. Brethren teaching embraces male-led meetings to the extent that women are not allowed to speak publicly, even to pray out or announce a hymn in the 'open' sessions. And then there are the bits of Scripture that seemed to be ignored.

Incendiary Devices

Gerald takes the opportunity on one of the 'open question' evenings (well, open to the men anyway) to ask:

'We've been going through 1 Corinthians as a church,' Gerald says, 'but we totally ignored chapters 12 and 14.' There is silence in the room. 'Why? Why do we ignore it? What about the gifts of the Spirit? What about speaking in tongues?'

In his naivety, Gerald doesn't realise the incendiary device he has just set off in the room. Someone mumbles about the young people never being satisfied. Eventually one of the elders responds, explaining that the gifts of the Spirit, including speaking in tongues, are not applicable for the church today. They have been replaced by the Bible. Gerald would do well to remember that and to study the Word more.

Yes, thinks Gerald, *study the Word, but presumably not 1 Corinthians chapters 12 and 14!*

If that had been the end of it, maybe Gerald would still be in the Brethren church. But more follows. One of the best bits for the young people is the end of the morning meeting. The 'Lord's Supper', the 'around the table meeting', is full of posturing as far as Gerald can see, but the time afterwards is genuine and very much enjoyed. Everyone becomes 'normal', has good conversations and drinks cups of tea. The fellowship is good . . . Until the bread incident.

Having been up early to help open the premises, Gerald is hungry. The bread and grape juice are still on the table at the end of the meeting. Gerald reaches over and takes a chunk of bread. No sooner has the bread reached his mouth than there is a loud shout from one of the elders.

'What do you think you are doing, young man?! That is the Lord's Supper. Put it down immediately!'

'But it's not,' argues Gerald, 'It's just bread. We celebrated the

Lord's Supper earlier. It's just the bread left over.'

'Well, it may be just bread to you but I assure you it's the Lord's Supper. Put it down.'

Gerald isn't beaten. 'But Mr West, the caretaker, makes bread pudding from it!'

Most of the congregation have left the room by now, some out of embarrassment. Gerald quietly replaces the bread on the table. He is struggling to see how exactly this 'open meeting' is any different to the traditions of the Catholic Church where they believe in transubstantiation – that the bread and wine mysteriously turns into the body and blood of Christ. What the elder is insisting upon feels religious. And Gerald is beginning to see the difference between religion and real faith.

Within Gerald there's a struggle. It's not just this incident. It's the whole thing around women being silent. It's the views on baptism of the Spirit. *Church isn't what I think is should be,* he ponders. *But what should I do?*

Doing Nothing

What he does is nothing. And nothing proves to be enough, for now.

Bryan and Jennifer decide to move on. A little uncomfortable with the direction of travel spiritually, they travel geographically back to Jennifer's home church. They are Gerald and Anona's closest companions and are greatly missed. In later years, Gerald reflects on many friends lost, often on issues to do with church and the pace of change. He regrets the loss – but not the changes! Soon after Bryan and Jennifer's departure, Gerald and Anona take the youth group on a camping holiday. It's while they are away that there's a split in the church. By the time Gerald and Anona get back, they are faced with a choice: the Gospel Hall or the other group who have left. Based on the degree of grace and friendship offered, they choose the other group and begin to meet in Cobham Youth Centre, which has formerly been a chapel.

Gerald's new home, Ebenezer Chapel, is a place of comparative freedom after the strictures of the Brethren assembly. Although still based on Brethren principles, the new fellowship is not able to draw on the same group of travelling teachers and preachers due to the conflict with the original assembly. This means new faces and new freedoms.

Gerald and Anona are quickly building a youth group again. And with greater success; there is less of a disconnect between the youth meetings and the main meetings. Reading of them in the London *Evening Standard*, Gerald contacts The Forerunners, an American gospel group linked to Campus Crusade for Christ. Their arrival brings new teaching to Gerald. They teach the 'Four Spiritual Laws', one of which is being filled with the Holy Spirit. Together with a visit to the Billy Graham Crusade in London, these encounters are opening Gerald up to the fact that there is more 'church' out there than he has experienced or been aware of thus far.

As Gerald's awareness of 'church' across the country broadens, he's drawn back to the accident. The miracle of it all has not been lost on him over the years. It is now, a few years on, that he begins to understand something of the significance. Increasingly, he senses a purpose beyond his own. Along with Anona, he's beginning to see that God has a purpose for his church, that church is still relevant, and possibly – just possibly – they have a part to play in all of this.

Miss Kidd

'Young man, I have been praying for this area for thirty years. I know you're the answer to my prayers.'

It's Coffee Bar night at Cobham Village Hall, near the end of a run of a month's meetings for the youth of Cobham. Gerald has seen some success with this and a good number are gathered, when a diminutive Indian lady approaches.

She explains her name is Miss Kidd and that Gerald and Anona are most definitely the answer to prayers prayed over many years. She has been praying for a new church to emerge, a better reflection of Christ in Cobham: something effective, something truer to Scripture.

Gerald isn't sure how to respond. This is the kind of thing that happens in the books he reads – but not in downtown Cobham! But there it is. There is something about her words that causes Gerald to pray, to seek God to be that answer: for God to make of him what He wants him to be.

Gerald's adventure in faith is speeding up. His baptism at the age of 20 had been a further catalyst for Gerald to seek God more, to be more intentional in his faith. So Miss Kidd's arrival two years later is timely and reaches a receptive spirit.

But how to learn? How to develop 'church'? How to be the answer to Miss Kidd's prayers? Is church just a meeting or is it the people who are the church? If church isn't what it should be, what exactly *is* it to be? If church is people, why restrict 'church' to certain times on a Sunday? Gerald's mind turns over these thoughts.

Miss Kidd's influence continues. She introduces Gerald to Alan Kay, a local church leader, and invites them both to a conference about the state of the nation.

One of the guest speakers is someone called Roger Forster. God is about to answer a number of Gerald's questions.

5

Pioneering Church

Let's go back a bit in time.

Anona's diary tells us it is Friday 14 August 1964, on a windy beach at Broadstairs, in one of the windbreak shelters. Gerald Coates, the old romantic.

Actually, it's been quite a fraught day for Gerald. He knows he wants to ask Anona to marry him. He thinks she'll say yes. But that doesn't make the waiting any easier. He's jumpy on the coach journey down to the coast. It's a two-day holiday with their friends Bryan and Jennifer. Anona has no idea how special a holiday it will become.

Gerald and Bryan book into their room and go in search of the girls. Gerald gets Anona on her own. 'Let's find an ice cream,' he says.

A few minutes later, with the wind blowing rather more strongly than Gerald thinks is romantically appropriate, and with sand attaching itself to the remnant of his ice cream cornet, he asks the question anyway. The words stumble out in a bit of a flurry. Caught in the wind, they are gone in an instant. But Anona hears alright.

At just 16, it's young to get engaged. But this is her man. Of course she says yes.

Three years her senior, Gerald is ecstatic. This is the girl he loves. They will make a life together; they will have a family. Already forming in Gerald's mind are plans for youth groups, churches, preaching and more. Anona is to be his companion, his best friend, his lover.

They marry two and a half years later and honeymoon on a houseboat on the Thames.

Challenge number one is the house.

Tartar Road

Cobham is expensive. But a small terraced property in Tartar Road is available for rent. At least it is when they go on their honeymoon. Gerald's dad has bad news for them on their return. The house is now unavailable.

'The agent has had to take it off the market. The owner may be moving back.'

It's a crushing blow and one that Gerald and Anona struggle with. Rather than give up, they turn to prayer. This particular battle is one that begins to forge a joint prayer life. It develops tenacity and regularity in prayer. They begin to make it a habit of praying at the start of every day. And with a house to pray for, there's a certain intensity to those prayers!

Living in lodgings follows and, when the money runs out, with Gerald's parents. The words of Anona's father ring in Gerald's ears as he accuses them of presumption. 'Why should God look after you? Why are you so special?' The words are a challenge. Gerald and Anona pray again.

It's late one night at the store. Gerald is just fetching his coat when the phone rings. He's not sure whether to answer it – he may miss his train. But he answers nonetheless.

'Mr Coates?' It's the property company. 'We've got news for you. Tartar Road. It's back on the market. The keys are yours if you want them.'

From day one, their home has an 'open door' policy. Followed by an 'off the hinges' policy when it gets too full! Friends are always staying, always calling round. It becomes a centre for the youth group from Ebenezer Chapel. Life is good. Gerald is doing well at work. Anona is married and away from a troubled home. And the youth group is growing on a weekly basis.

It is a shock, then, to find that the elders of the church have other plans.

'Gerald, we're going back. We're re-joining the Brethren assembly.'

Stunned silence. What to do? Gerald and Anona can't go back. The restrictions would be too great. The youth group that has been established couldn't possibly fit in with the more restrictive policies of the assembly.

In fact, the assembly elders make it pretty clear they would not have been welcomed if they had tried.

So one Sunday morning, Gerald and Anona, along with three friends, Roger, Penny and Linda, find themselves in the front room of Tartar Road in what, somewhat by default, may have been one of the very first representations of the House Church Movement.

Roger, Maurice and Arthur

But Gerald is not alone. The conference with Roger Forster is about to show him that.

Although this first 'charismatic conference' gives Gerald quite a headache. Literally.

It has been an interesting journey already in Alan Kay's clapped-out van. Alan's an enthusiast in everything he does. Including the driving! Gerald has pushed his foot down on an imaginary brake on more than one occasion.

The driveway to the house is quite imposing and Gerald can't help but feel a little overawed. Upon arriving, they are told by a rather well-spoken man at the door that the conference is to be a time of fasting. 'We trust that won't be a problem to you?' he asks in his manicured accent. Gerald tries to maintain a fixed grin and enthusiastic tone of voice as he thinks of ways he might be able to get around the restrictions! Gerald drinks a lot of tea and coffee, so inevitably the fasting gives him a caffeine-withdrawal headache for most of his stay. Not the best introduction to the type of church he will be associated with for the rest of his life.

The well-spoken gentleman turns out to be someone called Maurice Smith, who leads the meetings and introduces Roger Forster as the speaker.

The conference is pretty much lost on Gerald. He doesn't understand the language (how do you go 'up to Zion' – and what is Zion anyway?). Songs are sung enthusiastically. Gerald keeps up the pretence, mouthing the words to choruses he's never heard before. He only speaks once, when asked to share his experiences of the coffee bar outreach.

By the end of the time there, Gerald is sure he's not coming back.

'Oh good,' he says, as he and Alan are told of the next meeting. Fixed grin in place.

And, of course, it is good. It is the way forward for Gerald. A way of learning more of what the Bible says about church. A way of developing friendships, many of which will last for years to come.

Alan is enthusiastic about the meetings, and Gerald goes along with him. Literally and metaphorically.

These early days are a time of exploration for Gerald. He has been enclosed within a denomination and now, for the first time, he begins to see regularly all God is doing in the broader

Christian sphere. Other speakers come across his path, each adding to and influencing the nascent theology of Gerald Coates. People like Michael Harper, who goes on to form Fountain Trust. Denis Clark, Jean Darnall, Cecil Cousen and Campbell McAlpine among others. And Arthur Wallis. There is something about Arthur Wallis. He doesn't speak in public particularly well. But he has something Gerald wants: he is clear on his church theology.

Unlike Michael Harper, who wants to see a renewal in the denominational churches, Arthur Wallis wants to see a new church for a new day. His writings are challenging and the more Gerald reads in magazines such as *Renewal* and in printed conference reports, the more he believes that this is the way forward for the church in the UK.

Published as early as 1956, Wallis's book *In the Day of Thy Power* is particularly challenging for a young Gerald Coates. Gerald is not a natural reader, but the challenge of this book means he gets through it in record time. This is different. This is new. There's open criticism of denominations and what they have become. There's an awareness of the Holy Spirit at work and a desire for revival. The Hebridean revival is described in some detail. And, in Wallis's words, there is an anticipation of something new. A new church.

How can God renew a denomination, with all its restrictions and trivia? Why not a new church, reflecting the church of New Testament times? The radical Gerald Coates is being awakened.

Friendships

Life is hectic. Still working at H.L. Reid, Gerald manages his evenings as carefully as he can. Anona joins him in running the 'house church', they do evangelism out on the streets of Cobham, then meetings, meals and prayer times with their friends.

And increasingly, meetings with other leaders who are

pioneering church in a similar way. Maurice Smith, despite his well-spoken manner, is down to earth. He sees things simply.

'It's to do with relationships, Gerald. We can all do "meetings", but meetings aren't what God has for us. I believe we are living in a new day. A day for new churches, built first on friendship and faith, not around tradition and dogma.'

Maurice is strong on relationships but also the need for each church member to have a personal life-changing relationship with God through Jesus Christ. Otherwise, the church is not really going to be effective:

'The last thing we want to end up with is an ineffective church. If you join a lot of people together who are individually a mess, all you end up with is a corporate mess! Can you imagine a group of non-swimmers all trying to save each other?'

Gerald nods along. If he's honest, he's feeling a bit intoxicated with the company he is keeping. Thanks to Miss Kidd, he seems to have been given a back-door pass into these men's lives. The sheer brilliance of Roger Forster's Bible teaching. The excellent networking and organisational skills of Maurice Smith and John Noble. Arthur Wallis' clarity on what church is and is not. And friendship. These men, seemingly older and more experienced, treat Gerald as an equal. Gerald's prayers at night often include his grateful thanks for these new-found friends.

Doing Church

Some of the teaching may be getting clearer, but it isn't clear to Gerald how church should actually look in terms of meeting together. A reflective Gerald of later years says, 'We didn't really know what we were doing at all!' The significance of their new church model doesn't show itself at that time. Gerald studies Wallis and others, but there's not much on the 'how to'. Much more on the 'why you should do'. It is alright saying church is people, and not buildings, but what exactly is a meeting meant to accomplish?

That first Sunday morning in the front room with Roger, Penny and Linda doesn't start that well. In preparation, Gerald has set out the bread and wine (well Ribena actually) on a coffee table in the middle of the room on top of a pure white tablecloth.

'What am I doing?' says Gerald. 'This is just repeating the picture in my mind from the Brethren.'

So with that, the tablecloth is removed, the bread and wine placed on the top of the sideboard, and the room returned to something looking like a living room.

These early experiments with church are pretty 'hit and miss'. But there is no doubt about two things. Firstly, they are on to something. This feels real, less 'stuffy' than the assembly, more genuine. And secondly, the group is growing. Gerald and Anona are bold in their evangelistic endeavours and the numbers grow weekly. One of the early joiners is a young Hazel Soan, later to be an accomplished artist with her own television programme.

Not everyone that turns up is ready and willing to learn. The comparatively new (to that time) teaching that God can speak prophetically is being misused. One bizarre Saturday morning sees a young man arrive at the door with a lampshade on his head. He says God has told him Gerald is to have the lampshade in exchange for the (rather nice) lamp stand in the hallway. Gerald declines.

The group is more than just a Sunday one. The coffee bar is still operating, and alongside the evangelism there is a natural friendship, which means there are visitors to Tartar Road pretty much all the time. Their friend Roger even moves in for a while. There's no doubt about who is leading this group. Gerald starts the meetings most weeks and regularly speaks from the Bible. He's honing his skills with this small group, and improving each week. He's discovering that when you talk about the stories in the Bible, you need to apply them. They are for living: for Monday mornings in the workplace; for the difficult family situations; for the local and the national. Scripture can help you to pray for your MP effectively. It means that as a local church you can have a say through prayer into worldwide events.

Gerald is learning. And one of these points of learning is the need to know the Bible well. He studies hard and reads widely. He's aware that if he has the responsibility to speak to others, he needs to take that responsibility seriously.

Those who've seen Gerald speak in later years may consider that his presentation seems spontaneous and without notes. What they don't see are the hours of preparation beforehand. Starting from these early days of house church, Gerald begins a discipline he still keeps to. He is thorough in his preparation. Illustrations are thought through; quotes are identified; everything is prepared comprehensively and prayed through. A thirty-minute talk has probably had at least a day and a half of preparation and prayer. The more he studies, the more Gerald is finding that he is in the slipstream of others who have gone before him. Not just people like Arthur Wallis, but going back further. Much further. He finds that in the eighteenth century revivals in the UK, the Wesley brothers, John and Charles, worked through groups in the home. House church isn't so new after all. Gerald is learning, growing, getting more excited as he goes along. If God has brought revival to this country before, why not again? And why not through a new expression of church in the home? Which, after all, is not so new? Following in the footsteps of John and Charles Wesley is not such a bad thing to be pursuing.

By Faith

Gerald is getting known as a speaker. A good communicator, he is adding Bible knowledge and his new understanding of church to his natural abilities. Typically though, the financial gifts for speaking are not too good. 'Take what's in the collection plate' is a standard offer from the churches he preaches at. But when that is a couple of shillings and a button or two, it hardly covers the bus fare.

A huge step is taken. If God is calling Gerald and Anona to be radical, and to build a new kind of church, they need to be serious.

'What do you think?'

'If that's what God is telling you, you have to do it,' says Anona.

'It's such a big thing though. What if we're wrong? What if the church doesn't grow?'

Anona smiles. She leaves Gerald to consider the answers to his own questions. Aware of his faith and passion, and despite the questions as to how they will live, Anona knows this is the right move to make.

Gerald leaves his well-paid job in the store. He's practical as well though, and takes two part-time jobs: one as a postman and one working in a petrol station. The petrol station owner doesn't much like Gerald, but admits that the only time the till takings correlate with the pump details is when Gerald is on duty!

Gerald and Anona have been reading some of Watchman Nee's books. The books have been recommended to them by John Noble, and Nee, a Chinese Christian who suffered severe persecution, is uncompromising in his teaching on church and ministry. Influenced by his teaching, Gerald and Anona decide not to ask for money as Gerald steps out of regular employment, but to pray and to 'live by faith' as much as they can.

Even in the toughest times, God is looking after this faithful couple. One time, they find their milk bill has been anonymously paid, and extra groceries delivered. Another time, Gerald has enough money for the bus, but not for the train journey afterwards, that will take him to his preaching appointment. As he gets on the bus, praying about what to do, an old friend approaches and gives him the money he needs.

As John Noble tells it, there is at least one occasion when Gerald and Anona take a bus together – Anona is asked to pay the full fare, and Gerald with his short stature and young looks is offered half price!

And he is short. Or compact! Maybe that's a better description of Gerald. So the first time he puts his postman's uniform on, it is a sight to behold. Enormous!

It is while working as a postman that Gerald manages to break his leg in an accident. Just the day before, he's signed up to a small insurance policy that ensures income throughout the time of recovery.

Small miracles. But a big God. And a God Gerald and Anona are learning to trust.

6

BIND US TOGETHER

These early leaders meetings with Maurice Smith and Roger Forster are reaping a good harvest, not least the occasional appearance at Tartar Road of some of these new-church pioneers. Impromptu meetings are called when Maurice visits. Ted Crick and John Noble are other occasional visitors. Gerald and John get on well. Their early meetings are the start of a lifetime's friendship. John has the knack, as Gerald puts it, of pasting a few shades of grey into Gerald's black and white world!

At a particular set of meetings arranged for Maurice Smith, a new couple walk in. Mick and Liz Ray are struck by the freshness of the meeting and continue to attend, eventually moving to be near Gerald and Anona. Another key relationship is in place as God begins to grow the fellowship.

A church style is developing too, very much based on relationships. Arthur Wallis has been teaching that the new church has to be different. To deliberately drop all the tradition and the dogma of the old. This appeals to Gerald. So meetings are relaxed, and in the home while it is still big enough. It doesn't have to be a Sunday meeting either. Often a midweek one is preferred.

Everyone is able to contribute to the meeting itself, reflecting perhaps Gerald's time in the Brethren assembly – with the key difference being that women are able to speak! Communion isn't essential at every meeting but the Bible is always prominent, with some sort of teaching from it on a regular basis. Worship is central too, usually led on an acoustic guitar and making use of simple newly written songs which are starting to dominate the new Christian scene from the mid-1960s onwards.

It seems strange to record it now, but a hand raised in worship was quite a discussion topic, even through to the mid-1970s. Churches split over the issue. Some church leaders saw it as a deliberate undermining of authority from church members. Church worshipers were beginning to explore this outward expression and, with an inherent Britishness, some felt extremely embarrassed at lifting hands and arms in worship. Many a church member felt their heart beating faster at the thought of a raised hand in worship!

Slowly though, such expressions become commonplace in churches such as Gerald and Anona's. People begin to respond to the words of the songs, to feel the need to express themselves more physically. After all, it is God they are worshipping and there is plenty in the Bible encouraging them to express themselves in all sorts of ways in worship.

John Noble's wife, Christine, is particularly helpful. She's artistic and creative. Gerald and Anona learn about expressive dance in worship, about the use of flags and banners. Most of the time, dancing in worship looks like skipping – what becomes commonly known as 'the charismatic two-step'! But Christine helps add further dimensions to creative worship.

The songs themselves, especially in these early days, also reflect the closeness of relationships and working together to serve God. It may sound a bit twee now, but 'Bind Us Together, Lord' was mightily effective in the early days of house churches, when typically churches had been more formal and slow to develop any kind of meaningful relationships or deep friendships:

Bind us together, Lord, bind us together
With cords that cannot be broken
Bind us together, Lord, bind us together
Bind us together with love.

Extract taken from the song 'Bind Us Together, Lord' by Bob Gillman. Copyright ©1977 Thankyou Music*

Gerald is a good teacher. The meetings are different. The fellowship grows. Without knowing it at the time, Gerald is pioneering a new kind of church. He's called it 'house church' but at this time has no idea he is part of a new house church movement that throughout the sixties and seventies sweeps through the nation, bringing a prominence to people like Gerald, John, Roger, Maurice and others. These are exciting times. But Gerald knows something is still missing.

A New Power

The taboo subject at the Brethren assembly had been baptism in the Holy Spirit. The Brethren teach that such an experience has been replaced by the Bible. It doesn't make sense to Gerald. He can't see that particular teaching anywhere in scripture. On the contrary, there are plenty of places where the Bible encourages him to be full and overflowing with the Spirit.

Gerald is an extrovert in worship – not afraid of making a noise. So, on his mail round, he will often be singing at the top of his voice, and with his new-found love for the Wesley revivals, usually Charles Wesley hymns. And that's when it happens.

'Finish then thy new creation; Pure and spotless let us be. Let us see our whole salvation Perfectly secured by Thee. Keryarunda – sadavoostoo!'

The bike comes to a halt. Gerald gets off. What was that? How did that happen? Gerald isn't sure. He's been lost in worship to the extent that he is in danger of not concentrating on the cycling. And then it happens. But what exactly? Is this the speaking in tongues the Apostle Paul talks about? It feels good. He tries out a few more sentences. There it is. Real enough.

Could he be making it up, he wonders? No. Surely not. He isn't that clever!

Gerald's friend John Carter is brought in for more advice and prayer. By the end of their time together, there is no doubting it. Gerald has been filled with the Holy Spirit. And, true to form, the whole world needs to know!

Perhaps more importantly, Gerald knows. He knows there is a sudden difference in his own ministry. The teaching from the Bible seems to 'live' more as he shares it. His prayers are clearer, stronger. They have a greater faith element to them. What has happened to him is so obviously supernatural, there is no doubt his faith grows as a result.

Over time, he begins to pick up on the fact that there is more to the baptism in the Holy Spirit than simply speaking in tongues. He re-reads the passages in 1 Corinthians, Ephesians and Acts of the Apostles. He recalls the conversations with John Noble and Maurice Smith. There's some serious study going on here. Gerald wants to know, needs to know, all that is available to him through the Holy Spirit. Teaching others on the baptism of the Holy Spirit follows as well. For many attending Tartar Road, this is completely new. Both the enthusiasm and the teaching! What has been lost in many denominational churches is finding its outworking in a house in Cobham.

Gerald is developing his own study times as well. Someone shares a picture with him, early in his ministry, of a river running through a land. The land around is full of produce – all he is going to accomplish. But the river is essential. He needs to bathe in it, drink from it. Specific days are set aside by Gerald as a result, to think, to listen to God and to pray.

The house group grows to the point where people are sitting up the stairs and through into the kitchen. Over the two years they meet in their home, a pattern is formed. An early postal round for Gerald, followed by a short sleep on returning to the house. Then study and visiting people. Evenings are meeting times, as well as developing a prayer, healing and deliverance ministry. Gerald isn't too sure what he is doing with deliverance ministry, but the Holy Spirit seemed to know what to do.

An early prayer session with Linda, a teenager who is struggling with many fears, is instructive. As Gerald prays quietly for the spirits affecting Linda to go, she screams. Her body goes rigid. She tries to scratch and grab at Gerald. And then, just as suddenly, Linda is quiet again. And free from her fears.

'You should have seen your face,' says Gerald.

'You should have seen yours!' is the reply.

Birth

Without a clear mandate or intentional move to create a house church, Cobham Christian Fellowship is born. And a journey is beginning that will help revolutionise the church in the UK.

In fact, even the name 'Cobham Christian Fellowship' is a result of necessity and pragmatism rather than anything intentional. Barclays needs a name on the account when the first bank account is opened. Gerald and Anona come up with the name on the spot! It isn't just the fellowship that is born. Gerald and Anona's first son, Paul, is born in 1968, and two years later Simon arrives.

Eight years later, there is another surprise blessing when Jonathan enters the world!

Faith for living with a growing family brings its challenges. Gerald has to leave the postal job as the work of the church grows. There are times when there is no food on the table, no presents at Christmas and a lot of prayer for answers.

Short-term answers become commonplace, as God provides for immediate needs. A bill paid here. A parcel of food left there. The gift of an old Hillman Minx to drive. But Gerald is to learn that God can answer in more organised ways as well. Howard Pearce is one of the church leaders. He picks up on the fact that Gerald and Anona are struggling financially and proposes to do something about it by way of a regular church income. This seems to be somewhat opposed to the lifestyle Gerald and Anona have been pursuing in faith and Gerald protests at the proposal.

'You say you have left it with the Lord?' says Howard. 'Well, perhaps the Lord has left it with us!' And so a salary, initially of £10 a week, begins.

There's an increased church structure here as well. Gerald is a good speaker but he's prone to exaggerate. He doesn't check out all his stories. If he's to grow as a leader, there needs to be accountability. Mick Ray and David Taylor step up to help. As a result, Gerald doesn't get things all his own way. He shares with some excitement the fact that he has invitations to speak in five different nations. He's fully expecting Mick and David to rubber-stamp his travels. But they don't.

'Right now, Gerald, we want you here in Cobham,' says Mick. 'There will be time to travel but we feel we need you here right now – and you need us!'

As Gerald walks home that night, he's fighting the decision in his mind.

'How dare they! Don't they know what God is doing in my life?'

But it's because they know that they restrain Gerald from trying to do everything at once. A restraint that Gerald begins to appreciate over time.

Local preaching is encouraged, though. A young Steve Clifford, later to be General Director of the Evangelical Alliance, remembers Gerald turning up at London Bible College to speak to the students 'with a Bible in one hand and a tambourine in the other'!

It's testament to Gerald's speaking ability that Steve remembers those visits so well: 'I was impressed by the clarity of the message from this slim, impeccably dressed young man. And by the freshness of it all. This was different. It was exciting, attractive church.'

The impression is such that a few years later when Steve and his wife Ann are seeking God for direction, they consult with Gerald and then join him in the work at Cobham, where they quickly become leaders.

At the time Cobham Christian Fellowship is being established, there is sadness too. Both Gerald's father and mother die comparatively young, and are not to see their son pioneer something that would no doubt have made them proud.

With a little of the furniture from Gerald's parents' house and a financial gift from a friend, after eight years, Gerald and Anona are able to move out of Tartar Road to a slightly more spacious house at 52 Between Streets.

Growth

Once the doors have been taken off their hinges at Tartar Road in order to get as many into the meeting as possible, it becomes apparent that it is time for the church to move on as well. Starting in a room above a Christian bookshop, the Fellowship soon migrates again, and by 1973 they are at Ralph Bell Hall. Forty-plus people are now gathering at the regular meetings, held on a Thursday night. They are open times of sharing, still borrowing from Gerald's experience with the Brethren, no matter what he might say about this being new church!

Most people in the Fellowship are young, with the honourable exception of Miss Kidd. Visiting speakers are becoming common as the foundations of a new house church movement in the UK begins to take shape. Mike Pusey, a Baptist minister from Farnborough, who is making waves with his teaching on what 'church' should be, is a regular. Maurice Smith introduces Gerald to George Tarleton, a radical preacher who is later to go too far in his teaching, ending up as a 'Christian Anarchist', bereft of what would be seen as a mainstream evangelical faith.

There is an early international influence in the church, too, as Gerald links up with some of the pioneers in Argentina who are experiencing revival. From them he begins to learn how to 'administrate' a growing movement so that the momentum is not lost. Such influences are important, as there is no real model in the UK that these house church pioneers feel they can follow.

Meetings are noisy times, with the tambourine, chosen instrument of this new type of church, to the fore. Worship is still led on an acoustic guitar and new songs are arriving from the pens of songwriters such as Graham Kendrick and Dave Bilbrough.

With hindsight, a whole new style of church is being born. It doesn't seem like that at the time though. One could be excused for thinking it is rather messy, noisy and irreverent. There is little in the way of organised worship, with the open sharing format. It means that songs can be started in pretty much any key, and any song selected. Is there any truth in the story that once, the congregation began to sing 'He'll be coming round the mountain when he comes'?!

Gerald has long dropped the religious terminology of

'brothers and sisters', replacing it with the more secular 'ladies and gentlemen' as he addresses the meetings. But address them he does. Despite the open format, there is a central place for sharing from the Bible. Preaching is often with a prophetic edge, foreseeing what the preacher feels God is intending to do in the church or in the nation. Gerald admits that a lot of the time he is 'hacking stuff down', finding plenty of instances in the more traditional church of what he feels is irrelevant and religious. It makes for a slightly anarchic feel, and with visitors such as George Tarleton, this is all the more the case.

The old church format – the 'hymn sandwich', the formal address, and the formal dress – has gone. In its place, a relational meeting, open sharing and an excitement and anticipation that God is doing something new.

Relationships are strong. Gerald and Anona are building friendships that will last a lifetime. People are joining the fellowship because of friendship, and as the relationships deepen, people decide to stay, to regularly give financially, to give of their time and their energy, and not to move away with every job opportunity that comes along.

It's not just meetings of course. Becoming increasingly good friends, they help each other practically and financially. They work on each other's gardens. Those with skills help with damaged washing machines, service the cars, wallpaper the houses. They go on holiday together. There is a strong community spirit. As Steve Clifford puts it, 'We shared our lives and our lawnmowers!' As the church grows, friendships are such that the local population notices it. People can begin to tell when someone is a member of Cobham Christian Fellowship by the number of friends that go through the door, and by the way people help each other.

Relationships outside the fellowship are developing as well, none more so than Gerald and Anona's friendship with Peter and

Linda Lyne. Peter, a former teacher, is leading a house church in the Bristol area. The four enjoy each other's company and find it helpful to compare notes on their church experiences. After all, there doesn't seem to be much going on in the UK that *is* comparable.

This need to meet and compare what God is doing in similar churches is about to get some help from another direction.

The Fabulous Fourteen

By invitation, Gerald and others find themselves invited to discuss various aspects of 'new church' with like-minded leaders. Arthur Wallis has been gathering a number of men together since the early seventies. Known, self-deprecatingly, as the 'Magnificent Seven', men such as John Noble and Bryn Jones, as well as Peter Lyne, have been brought together by Arthur for times of debate, prayer and prophecy.

'Gerald, it's Peter.'

Gerald recognises Peter Lyne's voice on the phone and they catch up on a few family matters.

'Listen,' says Peter, 'there's another reason for calling. Arthur and the team want to extend our group beyond seven by adding seven more. Would you consider joining us?'

It doesn't take Gerald long to make his mind up. One of the younger members of the new group, Gerald enjoys the fact that they take their self-deprecating title a little further, and call themselves the 'Fabulous Fourteen'!

Gerald feels a bit intimidated at that first meeting. Unusually quiet, he observes men of God older than him and more mature in their Christian walk, praying and worshipping in a way that is new to him. Sometimes they would sing in the Spirit (in English and tongues) for an hour or more. The prayers they pray carry a passion and power Gerald hasn't witnessed before.

It's a rich and potent mix of personalities. All established leaders in their own right, it makes meeting together – and particularly agreeing together – a problem. This is to surface at a later date, but in these early meetings Gerald is grateful to be there and to be part of such a group. Arthur remains very much the 'father' of the group but increasingly, leadership is moving toward Bryn Jones and John Noble.

For Gerald, it is a time of learning and of strengthening relationships. He and John Noble become firmer friends. Gerald and Hugh Thompson find themselves comparing notes on the need for more grace in the church, and in 1975, their co-written book *Not Under Law* results.

Purpose and direction, theology, and even a modern church liturgy are forming around this early desire to see God do something new in the church.

7

To the Nation

Gerald is excited. But isn't he always? This new kind of church really works! And Gerald is keen to spread the message.

Peter Hill, a returned missionary, starts to attend some Maurice Smith meetings. Peter is concerned about the moral pollution in the UK – it is noticeably more of a concern than before he had left as a missionary. He wants to do something about it and, whilst visiting his friend, the journalist Malcolm Muggeridge, proposes a campaign. It is Muggeridge who has the foresight to suggest that Peter should not be 'against' something but 'for' something. And so, the nationwide Festival of Light is born. A gathering and a march, not *against* the downward trend in society, but *for* The Light.

With Gerald as one of the organisers, 30,000 gather in Trafalgar Square in September 1971 and march to Hyde Park, where thousands more join their number. Malcolm Muggeridge addresses the crowds, American rock singer Larry Norman attends and Arthur Blessitt brings his twelve-foot wooden cross to the march, as he speaks of carrying it around the world to every nation. Followed two years later by Spree '73, something is stirring. At first, Gerald thinks he will not see the like of such crowds again, but back in Cobham the light is spreading, linking up with many more lights from churches across the UK that are also concerned for the state of the nation and are beginning to declare it publicly. Church is not intended for strangely designed buildings, but for the streets and the pubs. The nation needs to hear; the nation needs to change. And Gerald has his part to play.

Come Together

In 1972, Peter Lyne is invited by Jean Darnall to bring a startling new Christian musical to the UK called *Come Together*. Written by Jimmy and Carol Owens, this is different to the more formal choirs of old and has one key ingredient that is completely new – an open acknowledgement of the baptism in the Holy Spirit. Partly entertainment and partly a worship event, nothing of its like has been seen before. In the light of more recent history, it is pioneering a new style of worship through the doors of the more moderate churches. *Come Together* is welcomed by many mainstream denominations –perhaps in part because of its United States roots and the role played in the musical by the star of music and film, Pat Boone.

Unbeknown to many at the time, the force behind bringing *Come Together* to the UK is this small group of radical thinkers, typified by the gathering of those with Arthur Wallis. Men and women who are disillusioned with church as it has been are now calling the churches to come together!

Gerald adds his considerable energies to the administrative skills of Jean Darnall and Peter Lyne, and along with others takes it to the nation. David Taylor, Gerald's fellow leader at Cobham Christian Fellowship, manages the day-to-day administration.

Choirs of hundreds train together and then sing together in the large concert halls and cathedrals of cities throughout the UK.

Friendships are formed and news of this new style of worship and church become known within the established church by word of mouth, causing many a member of a congregation to consider whether they should move, in order to enjoy the kind of worship they have appreciated at *Come Together*.

It is unlikely Jean Darnall or Peter Lyne expected that *Come Together* would have quite the effect it has, but it acts as a catalyst, as a calling card for the house church movement. Over the next few years, as this and other initiatives take root in the UK church, many begin to leave their denominational churches and join this new phenomenon of house church.

Baptism in the Holy Spirit, rather than being seen as something no longer relevant to the church, is again being taught from the early 1970s. Among the Anglicans, David Watson in York and Michael Harper with his Fountain Trust movement are paving the way towards a more thorough theology of the Spirit. In many cities, gatherings of young people across the denominations are taking place, some of them directly out of the success of *Come Together*.

A further influence from across the Atlantic in the early seventies is the Jesus Movement. Based primarily among the hippie communities on the West Coast of the States, a new 'Jesus Revolution' is taking place. This is radical Christianity. A strong emphasis on the Holy Spirit and also on evangelism. The 'Jesus sticker' is born and Arthur Blessitt starts walking around the world with his cross – complete with the obligatory stickers!

Music is changing too. Even *Come Together* starts to be seen as rather tame, as Christians begin to embrace rock music and adapt it to the Christian message. New record labels are forming, and with them, introductions to a new generation of Christian rock musicians, many of them from the States, such as Larry Norman (with his one-way finger pointing to the heavens) and Randy Stonehill. In the UK, the first Greenbelt Festival, a Christian arts festival, begins in 1974 in a field in East Anglia and grows to become one of the largest events of its kind.

New Church Growth

Something is changing in the UK. Regularly Gerald, Arthur Wallis, John and Christine Noble and others are receiving invitations to speak throughout the UK. What has started in Gerald's front room simply because his leaders had returned to the Brethren assembly now becomes something others want to copy. Most weeks see at least one leader from another church joining Cobham Christian Fellowship for their Sunday meeting in order to see how things are done.

Gerald begins to travel more, speaking at many of the newly formed house churches up and down the country. Many are asking for more than friendship. They need help, guidance, direction. How is this to be achieved? One church at a time as far as Gerald is concerned. The first is in Rotherham. Hardly on the doorstep, but as a result, Gerald travels regularly to speak and to support the new leaders in the church.

By the mid-1970s, thousands are leaving their denominations, seeking a new experience of church through the house church movement, with its emphasis on relaxed worship, a loose format to the meeting and the baptism in the Holy Spirit. With a genuinely visible alternative for the first time, new churches are taking over their local community centres as they get too big for the home. As a result, many in each locality see with their own eyes that they don't have to put up with the complacent Christianity on offer in numbers of denominational churches.

A growing number of cross-city gatherings throughout the UK is supporting all this. At a meeting of around a thousand at the Friends Meeting House, a first launch into something bigger in London, Maurice Smith apologises that they are meeting there: 'I would have liked to have had you in my front room tonight, but we've got a bit too big.'

Meetings at Central Hall, Westminster, follow. Then the Albert Hall. Gerald has filed most of his papers and documents with Birmingham University. Among these papers are early minutes of meetings discussing the move to the Albert Hall. The excitement at the move can be read on the pages. Gerald and George Tarleton appear to be given most of the early leading of these larger meetings, with Maurice Smith and John Noble acting more as hosts.

From meetings in Tartar Road to the Albert Hall in less than fifteen years.

Apostles and Prophets

How is 'new church' supposed to run, though? Gerald and his colleagues in ministry may by now have something of a blueprint as to how the actual meetings run, but what is the overall church blueprint? How can the whole movement be taken forward? One of the key concerns for these new leaders and churches is the role of apostles and prophets. Many churches in the UK taught that these ministries had ceased (just as they had taught that baptism in the Holy Spirit had ceased). But if churches are to be clear in terms of direction and if new churches are to be established, surely the roles of the apostle and prophet are essential? And just as for baptism in the Spirit, where exactly does Scripture say these gifts to the church are no more?

As for prophecy, Gerald is already witnessing amazingly accurate prophecies from one of the Fabulous Fourteen, David Mansell. There is no way David could have been cheating in some way, knowing in advance what he is 'prophesying'. He also brings accurate words of knowledge to individuals, in line with the Apostle Paul's teaching in 1 Corinthians 12, opening up people's lives to the work of the Holy Spirit. Intriguingly, this is the area of ministry Gerald feels particularly called to operate in, to be a pioneer and spokesperson for God to the local and to the national.

Arthur Wallis is still gathering people together to discuss these kinds of issues. Often they meet at Fairmile Court, near to Cobham, and because of the proximity, Gerald soon becomes the co-ordinator for the meetings. Arthur is concerned about the (comparatively new and United States-led) end-time theology that teaches a lot about the Antichrist and signs of the times but little or nothing about a role for the church. Linked to this is the concern to further establish the church through the ministries set out by the Apostle Paul in Ephesians 4. These are stated as apostles, prophets, pastors, teachers and evangelists. Arthur and his colleagues are uneasy with the possible over-emphasis on some of these ministries but with the neglect of the apostolic and prophetic.

Prophecies and Dreams

Gerald's driving a car. He's driving along a stony road with many twists and turns along the way, hemmed in by big trees on each side. Eventually he comes to an open expanse of beautifully cut grass – and promptly drives right over the manicured lawns in front of him! He's performing handbrake turns and churning up the whole area. What a mess! All that beautifully cut grass churned up by the car.

It's a dream. He wakes and wonders what it is all about. Ron Wing is a friend in Canterbury. He's good with dreams.

'It's your current car, isn't it, Gerald?'

'Yes it is. How do you know?'

'I can see it in the picture God is giving me,' says Ron. 'It's a dream for now, for today. It's pretty clear. The road is your journey and the trees are other men trying to hem you in. The grass is religion. It looks so pleasant to the eye. But "all flesh is as grass" and the worst kind of flesh is religious flesh because it looks so neat and tidy!'

So that's it. Gerald is to drive right through the grass. The dream is to remain with him throughout his ministry.

Gerald first recalls a direct prophecy over his own life in the early 1970s from a leader of a church in Bath. He is told he will take the gospel of the kingdom to many nations. The concept of the kingdom of God is one that is used a lot by Arthur Wallis as well. Gerald decides he needs to seek God some more on this, and as he does so, there begins an awareness of God's kingdom and His outworking of that kingdom in the here and now that will stay with Gerald for the rest of his life.

Other similar pictures and words follow. People prophesy over Gerald, seeing him as having a 'destructive message' – complementing the dream (which Gerald has not shared) – but that despite the challenges, Gerald's ministry will be successful, much to the surprise of many awaiting the fall from grace!

It's worth recording that many did indeed expect a 'fall' for this outspoken, challenging man of God. Gerald has enemies because of the 'destructive' content of his message (often towards the established churches and denominations) and some have been awaiting the day his marriage falls apart or he is caught in some other kind of scandal. It has never happened. Others did indeed fall by the wayside, but Gerald has remained happily married and, by God's grace, free from many of the scandals that have affected other leaders in the church.

Dress Sense

It doesn't help that Gerald dresses differently too. Despite many of the leaders in the house church movement 'dressing down', Gerald tends to 'dress up'. There are no subdued suits in Gerald's wardrobe at this time. His personal style is 'loud'. A canary-yellow jacket comes to mind. Yes, really!

There is actually a written record of a conversation between Bryn Jones and Gerald where Bryn expresses concern as to how Gerald may be seen by others. Gerald accepts the mild rebuke, and the papers record that he intends to get rid of his blue stacked shoes and yellow shirt!

Many within the house church movement have reacted against formal suits, relating them to formal church, and dress down for church meetings. Not Gerald.

Arriving as a visiting speaker at a church, he is welcomed by a couple of leaders in jeans and baggy jumpers. On noticing Gerald's suit and tie – how could they not! – they ask, 'Where's the funeral, Gerald?'

Gerald replies 'Where's the jumble sale?'

If it isn't an outrageous suit, it is a leather jacket. Terry Virgo, who went on to form one of the most successful reflections of the new churches with the Newfrontiers group of churches, recalls the first time he saw Gerald in a Maurice Smith meeting in the early seventies:

I had been perplexed by a very youthful-looking guy at the centre of the meeting. He wore a leather jacket, had noticeably long hair, was thin and had the look of an adolescent. Why was he there at the centre with the leaders? At the end of the meeting, Maurice invited this young man up to speak and tell everyone about the forthcoming Festival of Light. His passion for Christ, his spiritual authority, his skill of communication took my breath away. Tears began to flow. The meeting came alive with the urgent passion for the nation that he was communicating – and he was supposed to be simply announcing the event! For the first time I was encountering Gerald Coates.

It is the attraction of the oratory that captivates many. Gerald's preaching could possibly be seen on occasions as mean-minded criticism of denominations. But it rises to be so much more – a picture of what God's kingdom can be, what church can be. All delivered with that passion and authority.

And stories. So many stories. With Gerald, there's always a story to emphasise a point. And sometimes a story just for the sake of it!

Gerald enjoys the jokes too. At one time, he is touring and telling a particularly funny story from South Africa. John Noble decides to play a trick. As John says:

I was due to speak at a conference the evening before Gerald. I told the people that I was about to tell them a story which would be the one Gerald was bound to tell the following evening. I encouraged them not to laugh when he finished. Sure enough, he launched into the South Africa story only to be met at the end by a wall of silence. I don't think he ever forgave me.

Kingdom Theology

Gerald doesn't just knock the established church. Mentored by the likes of Arthur Wallis and Maurice Smith, he begins not just to understand the role of the church, but to preach it. What becomes known as 'kingdom theology'.

Set against an expectancy of a global outpouring of God's Spirit, Gerald begins to teach that church is not the whole, but is an important part of God's purposes. And God is bringing about his purpose through the church. There is a re-establishing of ministries such as the prophet and the apostle, and the direct result of this is a strengthened church. Unbound by tradition, the church will be relevant to society, without losing its cutting edge. Accompanied by a visible outworking of the Holy Spirit in meetings and on the streets of the nation, the church will become wholesome and attractive.

God's kingdom will change the United Kingdom. God's people will be open and honest with each other, having thrown off their religious masks. There will be no settling down. The church will pioneer again in the UK.

And there it is. The word 'pioneer'. Gerald writes about it a great deal in his later books, but he is beginning to think it and preach it as early as the mid-seventies.

8

DIVIDE AND MULTIPLY

Life is good. Gerald is enjoying all God is calling him to do. He is speaking at many churches around the country, learning as he goes a fresh doctrine of the church – one that sees a triumphant church, revival, new churches, and new moves of the Holy Spirit. And all in close relationship with others.

Gerald values those around him. Friendships have grown and continue to grow.

But the letter changes all that.

The Letter

It's October 1976 and Gerald is cleaning his beloved Vauxhall Victor when the postman arrives. There's one letter he doesn't recognise. A handwritten envelope, but a typed photocopied letter inside. It's from Arthur Wallis.

The sponge drops from his hand as he reads:

Most concerned with regard to the extent of the misuse of "grace" among the London brothers . . . feel that grace is being used to cover up licence among you . . . serious misgivings regarding a number of trends in your ministry . . . concern that there may be a demonic or worldly ambitious spirit at work . . . With regret, have no choice but to separate from you and end our covenantal relationship.

There has been some disquiet among the Fabulous Fourteen and, with regard to George Tarleton, some substantial theological concerns. Arthur and Bryn Jones have handled the issue of a brother who has admitted to a significant sin without consulting the other members of the group.

But to actually separate? The contents of the letter seem quite extreme and out of the blue. Gerald finds it hard to comprehend. He hasn't see it coming.

Gerald's style is fairly confrontational, and it may well be that on occasions, when he thinks he is having a good debate, others among the Fabulous Fourteen see it differently. For instance, he speaks openly about sexual issues such as whether it is okay for Christians to masturbate. This may have seemed fine for discussion as far as Gerald is concerned, but perhaps Arthur thinks differently. Of an earlier generation, and with a strong disciplinarian upbringing, it is unlikely Arthur would have chosen to engage in such discussions.

Then there is John Noble. Not just meeting in a pub, but sipping a pint as the church worships together. Again, perhaps hard for Arthur to comprehend.

Maybe Gerald's book written with Hugh Thompson was another stumbling block. Called *Not Under Law*, it sets out an excellent grace theology. But the application and style is quite controversial. To suggest that getting up early to study scripture can be legalistic and in the same category as keeping your hair short may not have been the best way to present the doctrine of grace.

Nevertheless, Gerald hasn't seen this coming. He goes inside, makes a strong cup of tea, and prays.

With hindsight, Gerald feels that Bryn Jones may also have been a co-author with Arthur on this. Bryn was from a stricter Pentecostal background, whereas a large number of the Fabulous Fourteen (later extended to twenty and including Terry Virgo, among others) came from Brethren or Baptist backgrounds, and tended to view things quite differently. Bryn had not been totally in favour of the expansion of the Magnificent Seven to the Fabulous Fourteen and his attendance at the meetings had dropped off. His move to a more exclusive kind of house church could already be seen at this time. Perhaps in Bryn's mind, the separation has already happened. Maybe for him, it isn't as cataclysmic as it feels for Gerald.

Looking Back

When you look back and read some of the papers and minutes of the early meetings of the Fabulous Fourteen, it's not hard to see the tensions. Bryn's lack of attendance is an issue. So is the 'sin' of one of the brothers and the way it is dealt with. There was clearly also a difference in emphasis in how the Fabulous Fourteen's meetings were seen. Gerald and others referred to them as 'workshops'. This was very different to the increasingly covenantal language that Bryn Jones is beginning to use at this time, reflective of his Harvestime movement, which later became Covenant Ministries.

In late October 1976, the (mainly) southern brothers, including Gerald and John Noble, met together to decide what to do and how to respond to Arthur's letter. They noted that others outside of the immediate situation, such as Terry Virgo and Dave Tomlinson, were feeling uncomfortable. As a result of the letter, a general loosening of relationship with others is evident, beyond those strongly linked to Bryn Jones and the predominantly northern brothers.

And then, looking forward. In July 1979, there's a meeting

between the parties aimed at reconciliation. Gerald is there. Arthur has clearly softened and is seeking to get past 'the letter'. Bryn, who has been living in the USA for a short time, is less reconciliatory and is unable to pull back from any of the strong statements in the letter, arguing that because he has been out of the country he has not been able to observe any changes.

Friendships are renewed, but there is to be no further working together of what becomes two separate groups.

The Great Split Forward

Looking at it now, Gerald sees God's hand at work. He calls it the 'great split forward'.

Both groups prosper. Bryn takes Arthur with him, and in later years Arthur defers to Bryn rather than the other way around. David Mansell and Hugh Thompson join Bryn (perhaps surprisingly for Hugh, bearing in mind his co-authorship of the book that appears to have caused offence). Terry Virgo also links up with Bryn, before being released into his own apostolic ministry in the early 1980s, as Coastlands (later to become Newfrontiers).

Bryn's strength of leadership and superb preaching ensures success for Covenant Ministries. At its height, it becomes arguably the biggest and fastest-growing of the house church streams, and the Dales Bible Week leads the way in how to effectively run a Bible week. Gerald remembers Bryn's preaching fondly: 'The prophetic series Bryn gave at an early Bible week on Jesus' birth, life and death is one of the finest things I have ever heard!'

With Bryn and Arthur moving one way, Gerald remains in close relationship with many of the other brothers in the Fabulous Fourteen, such as John Noble, Peter Lyne, Graham Perrins and Maurice Smith. Their magazine *Fulness* is part of the outworking of their relationship. Started before the divide, it runs from 1970 to 1982, reflecting perhaps the high point in the new house church movement. In 1975 Bryn releases his own *Restoration* magazine, and maybe there are signs here of Bryn's intent to run his own show.

Fulness

Gerald's concerns that *Fulness* might fold with the competition from *Restoration* magazine are unfounded, and Gerald regularly writes for the magazine, as well as running a 'noticeboard' section in the middle of *Fulness*. This records some of the humorous happenings within the churches. For example, did you know the song 'There is a River' was written by Ruth Lake! Clearly Gerald has found an audience for his humour.

The magazines are 'arty' (from the influence of Nick Butterworth and Mick Inkpen, who would both go on to be successful children's authors and illustrators) and undated. Maurice Smith 'drips on' in a regular column and Gerald's contribution is prominent – and not just with his noticeboard pages. His strengths as a communicator come through, as do his particular emphases and passions. Articles on relationships figure highly, together with those on commitment and not settling down.

Fulness isn't the only magazine Gerald writes for. An increasing friendship with Peter Meadows, the editor of *Buzz* magazine, a more mainstream offering for Christians, leads to articles and interviews that bring Gerald to the attention of others.

Gerald's style of delivery when teaching and preaching is changing at this time. He has been chastised by Mick Ray, one of his leaders, for not always listening to people and being too ready to jump in with strong prophetic words. Gerald changes in this regard, both with individual prophecy and with the broader prophetic teaching. Although still bringing a strong message, it is flavoured with a little more grace than in the early years.

St Andrew's School

Things may be feeling a bit rocky as far as the national scene is concerned, but back at home, the church is growing. By the late seventies, outgrowing Ralph Bell Hall, Cobham Christian Fellowship next move to St Andrew's School. Now meeting regularly on a Sunday, the congregation grows quickly from around a hundred to more than three hundred. Gerald is leading the church and speaking on the first Sunday of each month, whilst being released for the rest of the Sundays for his increasing national ministry. A secretary is employed, and a room converted at Between Streets to deal with the correspondence – as many as forty to fifty letters a week are now being received, as people around the country begin to experience the baptism in the Holy Spirit and acknowledge the need for a more authentic church relationship.

Not that Cobham Christian Fellowship doesn't have its critics. Local churches feel threatened. Despite Gerald's assurances that no healthy churches should be concerned, the fact is that many local churches are not healthy. Their back doors are wide open and people are leaving. This means that Gerald gets a lot of flak from local ministers. Where there is simple outward opposition it is relatively easy to deal with, but most of it comes indirectly, in the form of side comments, allowing stories to spread, and leaving innuendos out there within their congregations. There are plenty of ways of ensuring Gerald knows that other local leaders are not happy, and of implying to congregations that all is not right with Cobham Christian Fellowship, in order to deter members from 'going over to the other side'.

An honourable exception is Anthony Delaney. The local Anglican vicar is a fan of all that is happening. Some years later, he and Gerald work together on a number of projects. Gerald helps and advises as much as he can, whilst being rather aware of the fact that most of his preaching is not favourable to the Anglicans. Today Anthony is a broadcaster on Christian radio and leads the Ivy Network of churches in and around Manchester.

There's no doubt that Cobham Christian Fellowship is well known by the time they start meeting at the school. The church is having a significant impact on the local community, it is mentioned regularly in the local press – both good and bad press – and Gerald even experiences it at the local newsagent.

Gerald's at the counter, chatting to another customer. The man asks what Gerald does for a living.

'I'm a church leader,' says Gerald.

'Oh my God! Ha ha! You haven't been converted by that bloke Gerald Coates have you?'

All said with a degree of enthusiasm and in quite a loud voice. Others are looking on.

'Erm. I *am* Gerald Coates.'

'Oh. Oh, yes. Er, well . . . well, as long as you are happy, young man. As long as you are happy!'

And with that, he leaves the shop as fast as he can. Two of the other customers are trying not to giggle.

Despite opposition, Cobham becomes known as a centre for radical church. People from further afield are beginning to turn up to get a flavour of how house church works. And Gerald is being asked to speak at an increasing number of places. One of these places is Plymouth.

Noel

Over a period of time in the early eighties, Gerald visits the Plymouth church for a number of meetings, as well as spending time with the leaders. A problem arises with the main leader.

He is close to burn-out and Gerald invites him to spend time at Cobham to recover. Gerald calls a meeting with the leadership team in Plymouth to explain the decision.

'Great, when do we move?'

Clearly, they have misunderstood.

'No,' says Gerald, 'not a move! What are you thinking!'

It's meant to be a short sabbatical for the main leader and his wife.

'I wasn't inviting you all to move!'

'But why not?'

'What do you mean, "Why not"? You can't all move to Cobham!'

'Why can't we?'

'Are you serious!'

'Yes we are. We've already talked about it. We're all moving to Cobham.'

Silence from Gerald. This sounds pretty incredible.

But sure enough, around forty of the Plymouth congregation end up moving to Cobham in one of the strangest population migrations known to man.

One couple among the forty are Noel and Tricia Richards. They have already been writing some good songs, but the move seems to invigorate them. There is a new excitement about what God is doing, and a new passion in their lives. It comes out through their songwriting.

Noel's first album, *The Danger Line* is released in 1986. By then he is a prolific songwriter. Over the years, he has written many well-loved Christian songs such as 'All Heaven Declares', 'You Laid Aside Your Majesty' and a song co-written with Gerald called 'Great is the Darkness'. That first album points to the close relationship Noel and Gerald are developing, with a picture of Gerald on the inside lyrics sheet – appearing to pose as some sort of spy!

The relationship grows and Noel becomes both a close friend and his co-worker, a gifted worship leader and songwriter, putting into music much that Gerald is preaching. It's not unusual within the house church movement to observe relationships like this, notably Roger Forster and Graham Kendrick, Terry Virgo and Stuart Townend, Mike Pilavachi and Matt Redman.

Gerald has spoken into Noel and Tricia's lives many times over the years. He recalls one time in particular when he was at a leaders' conference and felt he needed to go and reassure Tricia that Noel was alright. It was an odd one for Gerald. Noel was away on tour and was due back that day. And Gerald knew that Tricia never worried about her husband when he travelled. So why bother with the reassurance? But Gerald was obedient.

'Tricia, I feel God wants to assure you that Noel is okay.'

She bursts out crying. It's not quite the response Gerald is expecting!

It turns out Noel has just landed and called Tricia to let her know it had been an emergency landing but he is fine.

Noel begins to travel with Gerald, opening the meetings in worship, drawing people towards a closer awareness of God being with them, and thus ensuring that when Gerald speaks, his words land upon fertile soil, soaked by the work of the Holy Spirit during the time of worship. Noel and Gerald's partnership is to continue for nearly thirty years of ministry together.

Kingdom Life

Along with other leaders in this growing movement, Gerald begins to gather people from across the nation. One of the first formats for this is Kingdom Life week. Held in Cobham and starting as early as 1979, this gathering under a large marquee reflects Gerald's prophetic edge in terms of wanting to teach, equip and prepare the church for all Gerald feels God has in store.

The title is Gerald's. By now he is captured by the whole concept of the kingdom of God. He sees the impact of the church on the nation. He sees what can be accomplished with action and prayer in combination.

And practically, he has to keep the churches he is now helping on the same page. What better way than a week together?

The preaching is sharp, pointed, humorous, critical, but most of all passionate. Gerald is into his stride as a preacher. Gone are the days when he's unsure whether he should be preaching at all. It's replaced with a confidence and authority as he speaks. Managed each year by the Cobham Christian Fellowship team, the numbers grow, and so does the size of the Kingdom Life site.

Although Gerald is aware of the already successful Dales Bible Week led by Bryn Jones, his initiative is separate and for slightly different reasons. It's a gathering of churches, as is the Dales Bible Week, but it's also setting out a different direction of travel. This is to do with relationships and creativity, friendships and purpose, but a looser, less structured gathering of churches than with Bryn Jones. There is a common purpose too: to see revival. Consequently, this part of the message from both camps is very similar, not least with many of the worship songs shared nationally.

Although Kingdom Life is smaller than the Dales Bible Week, with around two thousand attending at its height, there are not many Bible weeks that can announce that they have Cliff Richard singing there. In fact there are none, other than Gerald's event. At a time when Cliff is number one in the charts with 'We Don't Talk Anymore', he is to be found on a muddy site inside a giant marquee, singing to some very happy campers!

Kingdom Life finds a fresh energy from those that Gerald invites to speak. And along with other Bible weeks, it is bringing together the new church; those that have already joined the house church movement, plus those that are 'just looking'. Such Bible weeks become the new recruiting offices for the house church movement.

Kingdom Life runs from 1979 until 1984. At the height of the house church movement's growth, it is a real success; Gerald sees the value in bringing people together, in the strength of relationships, of worshipping together, of learning from the Bible together. Not just Sunday meetings, but weeks together. And in big gatherings. Bigger gatherings. Why not nationwide gatherings? International gatherings? Kingdom Life is the start, but it is not to be the last initiative of this kind.

9

A NATIONAL VOICE

The back pages of *Fulness* often advertise forthcoming meetings. These include what become regular events at the Royal Albert Hall. Having started at the Friends Meeting House, then Central Hall, Westminster, these regular gatherings once or twice a year feature various singers and bands, mixed with short talks and presentations – invariably featuring Gerald!

During the early 1980s, Gerald can be seen leading, appearing in and speaking at any number of Christian music events. He is often selected because of his ability to get the message across to younger people, with his strong youth group pedigree – he also tells good stories of course. This is again reflected in his writings in *Fulness*. It's hard to find an article that doesn't start with a story – a good way of grabbing someone's attention, rather than just teaching a theological point.

New Music

In the early days of the house church movement, there is something of a distrust of the Christian music industry. Considered out of date in the early days, it is then, when 'better' music begins to arrive, thought to be unstable, with Christians that have poor personal lives and no church base.

Gerald is uncomfortable with this distrust, but not sure what to do about it. And then there is that prophecy.

His name is Wayne Drain (yes really), and he is a worship leader and prophetic minister from the States.

'Gerald, I see tension in you,' says Wayne. He is holding up two tambourines by this point, one in each hand.

'You're a prophet and a bridge-builder. God is going to use you to bring the house churches and music scene together. The two need to move together in God's purposes.'

And with this, Wayne brings the two tambourines together, one on top of the other.

It's a public meeting and, as usual, Gerald feels a bit embarrassed about getting any attention. And he is not sure what to do about the word. There's been some contact with US singer and pioneer Larry Norman by this time, but not much else, outside of New Year concerts and celebrations at the Albert Hall. This is about to change.

Norman and Sheila

Birmingham. A cold, rainy day in 1982. Gerald is helping out at BBC West Midlands, interviewing guests for the 'God slot'. One of them is a music sponsor called Norman Miller. He's promoting a Jessy Dixon tour that is due to arrive in Birmingham.

The interview goes well enough. And afterwards they agree to meet up in London to talk some more about Christian music.

They meet at Harrods' restaurant one lunchtime. (Gerald at Harrods? Norman's paying!) Gerald and Norman start talking. And they continue talking. Eventually, after more than five hours in the restaurant, the management ask them to leave. In the meantime, a friendship has been forged.

'Gerald, I don't think we can leave it at this meeting can we? Do you sense God may be saying something here?'

'Exactly! Look how long we have been here! This is more than a meeting of minds. I genuinely feel God has joined our hearts in some way today. It's more than Wayne's prophecy. But that's part of it too.'

They make plans to meet again.

Norman is married to the singer Sheila Walsh. They have given up their own home in order to help invest in Sheila's singing ministry. And this is where it gets really interesting. The growing friendship Gerald and Anona have with Norman and Sheila is such that before long they are sharing a house.

Initially invited for four months, Norman and Sheila end up staying with Gerald and Anona for four years. Between Streets is getting too small: with rooms given over to the growing ministry, and now with Norman and Sheila arriving, something needs to give. But the next move surprises even Gerald.

It is Norman and Sheila who first suggest it. Instead of them paying rent to Gerald and Anona, why don't both couples take a joint mortgage and buy something bigger? The 'bigger' is somewhat larger than even Gerald has dreamed of.

Clive House. Named after Lord Clive of India. Four floors. Fourteen rooms. A separate stable block for offices. Huge! As Gerald and Anona drive up through the gateway to take possession of it in 1984, their old Ford Capri arriving outside the grand entrance to the house is a somewhat incongruous picture.

Gerald is buzzing. The house is a reflection of all God is doing. Far more than Gerald and Anona might have expected. God is good at multiplying blessings. And there is no doubt in Gerald's mind, with the miraculous way this purchase has gone, that God is indeed blessing. As it says in the Bible in Luke 6, this is a moment of 'overflowing blessing'. As Gerald and Anona have given sacrificially into the ministry over the years, so God has turned it around. And there, in front of them, is the result of that overflow.

'Can you believe this?' says Gerald, looking up at the high, ornate ceilings.

Anona smiles one of those gentle smiles. She's thrilled with all God is doing in their lives, and proud of the part her husband is playing.

It is to be a wonderful time for both couples. Gerald's increased influence in the UK churches and Norman's connections in the music industry lead to some interesting guests. Cliff Richard of course. Larry Norman stays. Mike Read, the DJ. Even Mervyn Holland, the great grandson of Oscar Wilde, pays a visit, Clive House having been the former home of the judge who sentenced Oscar Wilde. The comment from Mervyn Holland has stayed with Gerald and Anona: 'Your lives are far more interesting than that of my great grandfather!'

The Banquet

With Norman and Sheila in residence, Gerald is exposed to many more within the music industry and this leads directly to The Banquet. Initially at Wembley Arena, and described as 'a feast of rock and praise', it is an immediate success, leading to a UK tour. Just as the house church movement distrusts the Christian music industry, there has been some resistance in that industry to what they see as the 'young upstart' in the form of praise and worship albums. These albums have been initiated through the various house church Bible weeks in the UK and grow on from there to create a whole new genre of music.

The Banquet tour brings the two together. Day one at each venue is for Christian bands and day two for praise and worship. It is a clear success. Larry Norman sings, as does Sheila Walsh,

Dana and Bryn Haworth. It is helped by an appearance from Cliff Richard. Sue Barker, the tennis player and television host, arrives with Cliff and is particularly struck by the praise and worship day, not wanting to leave.

Evenings such as The Banquet are all the more powerful because of Gerald's artistic nature. He frequently discusses the content of his talks with John Noble's wife, Christine, with her gifting in art and drama. As a result, Gerald's talks are often interlaced with powerful dramas and acted illustrations which, as John Noble recalls, result in some amazing and heart-searching moments.

Gerald remembers one in particular, relating to the Prodigal Son. That night, many Christian prodigals return to a living relationship with their Lord and Saviour.

Protest and Proclaim

A friend of Gerald's has a prophetic picture for him. In the picture, Gerald is wearing a dark suit. His hair is parted conventionally and he's carrying a briefcase with important papers in it. This is to be a significant moment, says the woman who shares the picture. Gerald can't quite work out what is meant. The lady who has the picture has proven to be accurate with prophecies in the past, but this doesn't seem right. Gerald never wears anything but bright-coloured suits and never parts his hair normally, preferring a considerable amount of hair gel in order to spike it up; his own attempt at relating to younger people (it is the Punk era, after all) and perhaps reflecting his desire to look younger than he is.

Gerald is now a regular 'call-up' for radio and television stations wanting a quote. And the more he is involved of course, the more well-known he becomes. Danny Smith contacts him. Danny has been involved in the 'Free the Siberian Seven' campaign, seeking release for persecuted Christians in Russia. Out of this is born the Jubilee Campaign. Gerald joins the campaign and, working with

MP David Alton, raises concerns for prisoners of faith around the world, garnering the support of more than one hundred MPs along the way.

Valeri Barinov is a prisoner of faith. After several arrests and imprisonments, he is allowed to leave Russia and enough funds are raised for Valeri and his family to book a flight. But Danny is nervous. He isn't sure he can be there when Valeri arrives, and others want to use the release for their own political ends. Gerald agrees to cancel his meetings and ensure that he is at Heathrow to collect Valeri.

Because the case is so high-profile and there is a need to ensure Valeri's acceptance through the UK border controls, Gerald puts on a dark-coloured suit and forsakes the gel. Placing the release papers in his briefcase, he heads to his car. It is only as he is driving towards the airport that he recalls the prophetic picture. He laughs out loud at how God once again has surprised him. The picture brings him assurance that, despite the political pressures and external influences, today is going to be just fine.

And it is. Valeri and his family are safely collected and they settle in the UK.

The success of this protesting and proclaiming, managed through the Jubilee Campaign, helps Gerald formulate another essential initiative. AIDS has arrived in the UK, and the fear and prejudice that comes with it makes it hard for anyone to formulate a medical and sociological approach to it. Dr Patrick Dixon belongs to a related church. He and Gerald begin to develop what becomes known as ACET (AIDS Care Education and Training). The charity leads the way in home care for AIDS patients, and within a decade has four major offices, employing thirty staff, and reaches around the world with care and education programmes.

The Rock Gospel Show

The BBC makes a bold move in 1984.

They have seen, over the years, an increasing interest in Christian music, and occasionally such music entering the secular charts. As far back as the Festival of Light and 'Light up the Fire' by Parchment, the crossover has been identified. By the 1980s, After the Fire and Bryn Haworth are making inroads into the charts and Cliff continues his success, sometimes with overtly Christian material ('The Only Way Out' and 'Little Town' for example, plus a duet with Sheila Walsh: 'Drifting'). Recognising this, the BBC ask Sheila Walsh to head up a new programme, *The Rock Gospel Show*. She is joined later by Alvin Stardust, who has found faith as a Christian at one of Gerald's meetings. The programme runs for two years and has a couple of spin-offs with Christmas and Easter specials. Artists appearing include Cliff Richard, Larry Norman, Russ Taff, Paul Jones and the London Community Gospel Choir.

Gerald, involved in helping Sheila, finds himself defending her on more than one occasion from Christians who think she has executive control of the programme and what is said on it. Of course she hasn't. The BBC doesn't always get the programme right in terms of content and Christian message – particularly as far as some of the more conventional Christian public are concerned. But the programme is pioneering in terms of getting a gospel message out on a television station not known for its positive views towards Christianity.

Getting Known

Gerald is getting known as a broadcaster. His links with Sheila and Norman and the work with the BBC result in other opportunities. Gerald is asked to speak on a number of culture programmes with Melvyn Bragg, discussing what 'faith' is. He is on Joan Bakewell's programme, as one of her presenters, leading debates on Christianity and atheism. He's invited onto a number of Sunday morning TV shows, as well as numerous appearances on the BBC's *Songs of Praise*. He's a guest on Radio Four as they debate witchcraft, and on the BBC2 programme *Friday Report*, as they investigate the evangelical church. It's on this programme that Gerald comes through at his best. The interviewer, Michael Delahaye, opens up the conversation.

'You evangelicals are all into show business, aren't you?'

'I'm not sure what you mean?' says Gerald.

'Well, your whole approach is American, isn't it? More like show business?'

Gerald smiles.

'Have you been down to your local church on Sunday recently? Grown men dress up in long gowns, carry around handbags that emit smoke, bow down to tables covered in coloured cloths and light candles either end. We couldn't possibly compete with that!' Delahaye nearly falls off his seat, laughing.

In Christian circles, too, this revolutionary preacher from the house church movement is starting to speak on a broader platform.

In 1979, with support from Clive Calver, then General Director of the Evangelical Alliance, Spring Harvest is born. It might be seen as an evangelical church answer to the charismatic Bible weeks such as the Downs Bible Week and the Dales Bible Week, both of which are underway by then. At first, the leadership team of Spring Harvest is careful not to invite anyone who might upset the delicate balance between Christian conservatism and the new church wing.

Over time, the doors open wider. Terry Virgo speaks for several years, particularly at the morning devotions. And Gerald is there too. A speaker at first, invited by Clive Calver, he's later asked onto the organising committee. His involvement becomes so great that he begins to get letters of complaint when some particular item or talk doesn't agree with someone's own theology – their assumption being it's Gerald's event.

Jeff Lucas

Gerald has further input into Spring Harvest over the years in the form of two key prophetic words for Jeff Lucas.

Jeff is from an Elim Pentecostal background and has been in the States for a while. Pioneer makes him feel welcome on his return, and he works with Roger Ellis at Chichester for a while.

At a Pioneer leaders' conference, during the afternoon, Gerald says to Jeff that he has a prophetic word for him, which he's going to bring publicly in the evening meeting.

Cue a nervous Jeff!

And he has reason to be nervous. At the evening meeting, Gerald produces a jester's cap and a shepherd's staff. He calls Jeff forward, places the staff in his hand and the cap on his head, stands back and says nothing. People in the conference are laughing by this time. Jeff isn't so sure. He's embarrassed.

'Jeff,' says Gerald, 'God has called you to be a fool for Christ. Your call is to humour. And your call is to shepherd. God gives you both. The hat and the staff. You are to be who you are!'

Jeff's finding it hard not to cry by this stage. Not now with embarrassment, but with relief. He's been asking God what his calling is. He believes it includes humour, but is concerned he will be seen as some sort of lightweight if that's all it is. But the prophetic word that night is a release to him to be who he is meant to be. He doesn't have to be someone else. He can be himself!

Later, an actor reminds Jeff that in the Shakespeare plays, the jester gets to have special access to the king. Jeff can enjoy a close relationship with the King of Kings.

As for the staff, part of the prophecy is that Jeff should carry it around as a sign of dependency. So he does. It is over six foot in length and made of carved wood. Hard to miss. And difficult to explain. Eventually, United Airlines manage to lose it on a flight. Jeff isn't too disappointed.

Gerald has another word for Jeff.

Passing him in a meeting one time, Gerald jumps back as he sees him.

'Oh! God has just given me a word for you! Something is going to happen that is not on anyone's agenda. Something unexpected. Watch out for it. It's going to happen in the next two to three weeks.'

Two weeks later, the current committee overseeing Spring Harvest resign and ask a new team to take on the leadership, which includes Jeff. It's completely unexpected. And Spring Harvest continues the growth that has been faithfully nurtured by its founders.

Ichthus

With the break-up of the Fabulous Fourteen, Gerald finds the need to form new and stronger friendships. He joins with John Noble and Dave Tomlinson (who had for a time been part of Bryn Jones' Harvestime movement). The three meet regularly, a product of which is the Festival Bible Week, which starts in 1983 at the Staffordshire Showground. Unlike other Bible weeks, this has a more laid-back and creative feel, reflective of its leaders. Alongside Gerald speaking on the 'Ethos of the Kingdom', there are presentations of art and dance, and even a set of seminars on gardening!

One of the other key influences for Gerald has been Roger Forster, leader of the Ichthus group of house churches. Roger has been on the scene for a while, sharing meetings with Arthur Wallis as early as the 1950s. On one occasion, at a conference in 1958, Roger comes prepared to present a 49-page thesis. This is one serious scholar!

And that's exactly what Gerald needs. Gerald is the first to admit he's no theologian, but there is a need to be clear on his beliefs, especially with the new churches that are forming. From the earliest meeting promoted by Miss Kidd, Gerald and Roger get on well together. They often speak at each other's churches and they share conference platforms together. Gerald is a guest at many an Ichthus conference over the years.

Roger's theological stance has an emphasis on man's choice to follow God's ways, with a strong focus on the power of prayer to change things. This is pretty much at one end of the theological spectrum for house churches, with the other end being a strong emphasis on the sovereignty of God – that God can and will always have the final say, irrespective of what we do. This second view is held more strongly by leaders such as Bryn Jones and Terry Virgo.

Gerald feels at home with Roger. And with his theological views. The strength of belief that the church – and the individual – in prayer and action can change things, has led to Gerald being particularly active in his faith. Add that to a get-things-done-type character and a lot gets done!

Tozer

Alongside Roger's obvious influence is a more subtle one. Gerald is introduced to the writings of a fellow prophet from an earlier time. A.W. Tozer is an American preacher and author from the 1940s and 50s. He writes as he speaks – directly. There is a challenge to action, no quarter is given to any kind of Christian compromise and there is a call to a holy and prayerful life. This mix of action and prayer appeals to Gerald.

Asked in 2006 by Crusade for World Revival to write a chapter in a forthcoming book on a book or author that has impacted his life, Gerald chooses Tozer. He describes him as having such a winsome style that 'you barely realised that the sharp knife of God's Word had done its cutting work.' Gerald learns from him the need to avoid superficiality and quick fixes in his own ministry. Tozer makes Gerald serious. Serious about preaching the truth.

In a similar way to Tozer, Gerald is to find that saying things straight gets you banned from certain preaching platforms. But, like Tozer, it doesn't stop Gerald from preaching what he believes needs to be said in a straightforward manner and with a sharpness and boldness that occasionally causes the listener to take a sharp breath.

Tozer and Forster – a stirring combination in Gerald's life. His theology is the stronger for it.

Gerald's friendship with Roger Forster is also the genesis of one of the most far-reaching initiatives – perhaps Gerald's finest hour – the March for Jesus.

10

SETTING OUT THE MESSAGE

Before we get into the March for Jesus story, amazing as it is, let's look more closely at how Gerald forms his theology, and how this works its way into print and preaching. Stay with it. It may seem a dull introduction to a chapter, but Gerald's theology is nothing less than dynamite for the church. Many reading this may not realise it, but the theology that informs Gerald and others like him has permeated and permanently changed the church in the UK.

At the time the house churches are gaining momentum, theology in many churches in the UK is influenced by what is a comparatively new teaching along the lines that Jesus is going to come soon and quietly 'rapture' his church. This emphasis on the Second Coming and also on the geographical Israel and the Middle East means that the church is pretty much forgotten. At best, it becomes a haven for the persecuted, but is certainly not very active in the streets, offices, marketplaces and neighbourhoods of the nation.

God's not Finished with His Church

The idea that God has not finished with his church and that the church can have a significant impact on a nation was new to many in the 1960s. Arthur Wallis taught unashamedly at this time that denominational churches had failed, lost their way and blunted their edge, and that a new church was arising.

A new church – a house church movement – was indeed arising. From houses to community centres to converted warehouses, new churches were getting themselves on the map: developing community action, declaring the gospel, and seeing many converted to Christ.

It's a Saturday evening in one of the many Bible weeks and camps arising in the UK during the 1970s. Gerald is on the main stage and in full flow:

'God will not be tied to seventeenth-century language, eighteenth-century hymns, nineteenth-century buildings and twentieth-century religious inflexibility! God is changing His church! We are part of that change!'

There's cheering and clapping. Very few in that particular audience will have had a problem with Gerald's words. Those that stay loyal to a denomination are there because they feel they need the kind of spiritual top-up a Bible week can give. So they are happy to forgive the language Gerald uses.

Not so leaders in the denominations!

Gerald's early teaching is blunt, almost aggressive. He takes no prisoners. He attracts much criticism from the established church.

There is criticism from the press, too. Gerald recalls a particularly damaging article from the *Mail on Sunday* when he allows a reporter into his life for a few days. The reporter is pleasant enough in the interviews and at the meetings, but the resulting article is venomous and elicits more than fifty complaint letters to the newspaper – and Gerald has asked his own church not to write and complain.

Criticism from others is a price Gerald has been willing to pay in order to get God's message out by every means possible. And it doesn't stop his own criticism of denominations and religious practices.

Noel Remembers

There are many stories to illustrate the point. Noel Richards, Gerald's closest companion over the years, remembers one in particular.

They're in New Zealand – an early visit in Noel's own ministry. The night before, there has been an amazing meeting. God has moved by His Spirit and many people have been filled with the Spirit, others healed. Many stood worshipping with hands raised, singing out in tongues.

The next morning. Sunday. The same church building. Many of the same people. Noel arrives early to set up his guitar. Straight away he notices the difference in atmosphere. There's a big table in the middle of the stage with a white tablecloth on it and bread with communion wine. People are talking in hushed tones. Everything has suddenly become pseudo-spiritual.

'Well,' says Noel to the minister, 'Gerald's not going to like this. Not at all!'

Gerald arrives. He frowns but says nothing. After the time of sung praise and worship – which is considerably more muted because of the cloud of religion hovering over the gathering – Gerald is asked to speak.

His first comment on taking the floor: 'Of all the meetings that exist in the church calendar, this is the one that I detest the most. And this (he grabs the white sheet and yanks it off the table) doesn't help at all!'

There's a sharp intake of breath from the congregation. To make matters worse, Gerald then proceeds to break off a chunk of bread and eat it, as he explains further why remembering Jesus' death in this form is never intended to be some sort of religious ceremony. Some indignant people stand up and shout at Gerald that he is wrong to be eating the bread in this manner.

Gerald's response: 'We are all going to eat this bread in a few minutes; I am just having mine early!'

To Noel, this is 'classic' Gerald Coates. At his best when tackling the religious spirits that are found all too often in our churches and gatherings. Rattling the cages of those who hold as sacred the non-biblical customs that sadly exist throughout Christendom.

And as far as Gerald is concerned it is fine to rattle the cages. There is a new church that needs building: people, rather than bricks and mortar; a relationship with God, not a relationship with rituals and church services; new wineskins for a new Holy Spirit-anointed church. And a kingdom to establish.

What on Earth is this Kingdom?

That word 'kingdom' sticks with Gerald. When he first starts to talk of the kingdom it's a word that isn't used much. Only by Jehovah's Witnesses and vicars at funerals anyway!

The word kingdom becomes Gerald's watchword in his preaching and writing. The church is not the kingdom, but it is central to the kingdom. God intends to establish His kingdom – in contrast to the 'United Kingdom', which is, Gerald says, neither united nor a kingdom. And God intends to establish His kingdom through His church.

Gerald's preaching is not enough. The word has to get out there in as many ways as possible. Gerald the evangelist. Gerald the enthusiast.

There's interest from the mainstream Christian press. He gets to know the publishers at Kingsway. In 1983 *What on Earth is this Kingdom?* is the result. It's not the only book on the subject, but one of the first to get mass publication from the house church movement into the broader UK evangelical churches.

It's full of Gerald's stories, interlaced with teaching that is radical in its day. Gerald confesses that he has to say some 'hard things' (about denominations mostly) and as a 'vendor of words', he is keen to engage with and change those who read his words. Gerald is also, for the first time openly in print, talking of himself as a 'prophet', reflecting his strength in this particular gifting as set out in the Bible, in Ephesians 4.

Gerald says he's 'captive' to the world's greatest theme – that of the kingdom of God. Jesus speaks of it more than almost anything else. And the church is central to the kingdom, called to triumphantly usher in the age to come.

There's an obvious excitement in Gerald's writing. It's infectious as you read it. And for many, this is a new theology. But actually it's a very old theology. Many of the early Church Fathers would have shared Gerald's beliefs on the church. But with failure, a lack of revival and apparent inaction on the part of God, easier, less costly doctrines have arisen that don't need a successful church.

And Gerald is clear to point out that accepting that God has a plan for His church is indeed costly. There can be no sitting back in inactivity. The church has to move forward with relevance. This means that both in meetings and out on the streets of the UK's towns and cities, the church has to speak with a clear voice.

Gerald sees a growing kingdom, reflected in strong relationships across the church, based on honesty and even submission – a controversial word in the church at that time. It probably still is! And the challenge to the reader is to get on board with what Gerald sees God doing – making sure that they are in a church that is relevant, growing and active in bringing in this kingdom.

Kingdom Defined

In those same Bible weeks, Gerald finds himself often speaking on the kingdom – its ethos, its people, its effect. The kingdom is here now but there is a sense in which much of the kingdom has yet to be revealed. We need to have both a great joy that God is at work, mixed with a godly dissatisfaction that there is so much more to come.

We need to be unashamed about God and the kingdom, Gerald says. The kingdom of God is an absolute in an age when there is a dislike for anything that is certain. Cue one of Gerald's jokes. 'People say to me there are no absolutes today, to which I say, "Are you absolutely sure about that?"'

At Festival '83 and with the publication of Gerald's book at the same time, the message is even clearer. Personal transformation is not enough. It must be followed by corporate and social transformation. New churches and a new agenda. Broader than reform and deeper than revolution. Bringing in the kingdom of God will come about, not by a major moment in time, but by thousands of minor incidents. Every time we change a person or a situation by God's power and grace, we have seen the kingdom come.

The kingdom is both now and yet to come. As Christians, we live in that tension. But one thing it is not is just holding on, waiting for Christ's return. There's a church to build and there are nations to change!

Inheritance

Along with the teaching come the new songs. Many are kingdom-centric. Songs are making huge statements about the church coming alive. There are declarations of God's triumph across the world, such as in Dave Richards's song, 'For I'm Building a People of Power':

For I'm building a people of power
For I'm making a people of praise
That will move through this land by My Spirit
And will glorify My precious Name

Build Your church Lord, make us strong Lord
Join our hearts Lord, through Your Son
Make us one Lord, in Your body
In the kingdom of Your Son.

Extract taken from the song 'For I'm Building a People of Power'
by Dave Richards. Copyright ©1977 Thankyou Music*

It's not hard to see why the critics of Gerald and others are getting upset. It's not a big leap from the triumphalism of a song like this to arrogance, suggesting that some might think themselves to be *the* chosen ones who would form an entirely new community of God's people, excluding all others.

Theology is often carried in song. It has been so through the centuries. The sixteenth-century reformer Martin Luther wrote many hymns to ensure people remembered doctrine. Charles Wesley did the same for the eighteenth-century revival in Britain, enabling those who could not read to remember biblical teaching. There is the same principle at work within the house church movement. Dave Bilbrough's song 'An Army of Ordinary People' becomes the calling card for many new churches, declaring to those in denominations: 'this is it – come and join us!'

An army of ordinary people,
A kingdom where love is the key,
A city, a light to the nations,
Heirs to the promise are we.

A people whose life is in Jesus,
A nation together we stand;
Only through grace are we worthy,
Inheritors of the land.

A new day is dawning,
A new age to come,
When the children of promise
Shall flow together as one.
A truth long neglected,
But the time has now come
When the children of promise
Shall flow together as one.

Extract taken from the song 'An Army of Ordinary People' by Dave Bilbrough. Copyright ©1983 Thankyou Music*

As you read the words, spot the theology. Ordinary people inherit all God has for them. It's a new day. New truths have been found. There's a new unity on the way. The church will be a light to the nations. This is kingdom teaching in song.

There is no doubting the effect that this kingdom teaching has had on the church as a whole in the UK. Along with other pioneers of the house church movement such as Terry Virgo, Bryn Jones, Tony Morton and Stuart Bell, the whole emphasis of God's kingdom and a triumphant church has transformed the local church we see today. Instead of local congregations 'holding on' until Christ's return, they now pray and act differently.

It's hard to over-emphasise the enormity of the effect of this theology on daily church life. David Matthew, one of the early leaders with Bryn Jones, set out a graph in *Restoration* magazine of expected kingdom growth, from restoration of the work of the

Holy Spirit through to the complete restoration of all things at Christ's return, with the church central to that return, as the bride of Christ.

This kingdom or 'restoration' theology of the triumphant church is firmly formed in many a local church today, and the results are significant.

As churches have moved onto the 'front foot' in terms of evangelism and community work, they have grown. As they begin to believe that God intends to bring in His kingdom and that the local church has its part to play, there is a subtle shift in attitude. A different mindset brings a different result. Prayer is more focused. Vision for the church is sharper.

There are links from this teaching to the March for Jesus, the Alpha Course and the new strains of evangelical Anglicanism in today's church. There is a significant inheritance from Gerald and his fellow pioneers to the church in the UK today.

Pioneers and Settlers

A main theme in *What on Earth is this Kingdom?* is the challenge to be a pioneer rather than a settler. Gerald first picks up on this from another speaker, but it quickly becomes his own. The theme can be seen in embryonic form in early issues of *Fulness* magazine and it reaches its full version in the book.

We are called to be pioneers, says Gerald, but so often take the easy way out. A settler resists the cost of change; a pioneer embraces it. A settler is afraid of making mistakes; a pioneer is unafraid. A settler uses church language such as 'meetings', 'services' and 'constitution'. A pioneer uses kingdom language such as 'obedience', 'service', 'sharing' and 'God's rule'. A settler is predictable . . . You get the idea!

As Gerald is writing, he is clearly challenging himself. Never one to accept the 'norm', his phrase 'constant change is here to stay' has been a hallmark of his own ministry.

The book is a success. An early reference manual for the house church, it joins Ron Trudinger's *Master Plan* and later, Arthur Wallis' *The Radical Christian* and Terry Virgo's *Restoration in the Church* as required house church movement reading.

Further On

What on Earth is this Kingdom? is just the start. Through the years, Gerald will return to print to reinforce the message. Within a year, *Gerald Quotes* hits the press, supporting the ideas that surfaced in *What on Earth is this Kingdom?* and adding some depth to key issues. It's pithy and controversial (of course) in its quotes which are used to discuss various issues relevant to the church. How about, 'One of the reasons the church in Britain has failed to grow is quite simply because it is full of people who are extremely rude!'

Other books follow. The titles explain their content pretty well: *Divided We Stand? He Gives us Signs* and *Kingdom Now!* The latter, published in 1993, is primarily a reworking of *What on Earth is this Kingdom?* and is followed within two years by *The Vision*. By now God is moving by His Holy Spirit through what becomes known as the 'Toronto Blessing' and Gerald is keen to link in this revival among the churches with his expectation of a bigger work in the nations.

Most of Gerald's writings relate to this one theme: the kingdom. It has captured him. It has become the theme of his life.

Gerald is justly proud of his books. He recalls the thrill of receiving an advance copy of his first book in the post. Propped up on the kitchen table, it stayed there for a few days and elicited a smile every time he went past! For a schoolboy who was not particularly intellectual, he's grateful to God for the ability to write and communicate. His new faith at the age of 12, along with his discovery of a love for acting at around the same time, combined to take an 'ordinary boy' and make of him something different. Different – and controversial.

Controversy

Controversy is never far away from this outspoken prophet. In 1985, the church historian Andrew Walker writes *Restoring the Kingdom*. It's the story of the house church movement from a sociological standpoint. Well written, it later gets a makeover with some new material. Andrew has not checked some of that new material with Gerald, and as it connects directly to issues relating to Gerald's finances, this proves to be a problem.

The first Gerald knows about it is when he gets a phone call from one of his church trustees.

'Have you seen it?'

'Not this edition, no, but I'm sure it's much the same as the first edition.'

'You need to read it. Now.'

It appears Andrew Walker has interviewed someone who complains of Gerald 'milking the audience' for funds at a Bible week. Whether this is true or not is not the issue. Walker goes on to suggest that such funds may have been used to help Gerald with his personal house purchases. It is implied, not stated as fact, but there is no getting away from the implication.

Gerald has always been very open with his financial dealings and will never think of taking money for personal gain, a fact confirmed by his close friend, and successful businessman, Paul Williams. Paul and Amanda have been with Gerald and Anona from the early days. At no time can he recall Gerald asking for anything financially.

There's a stand-off between Gerald and the publishers. If Andrew Walker's revised book was to reach Christian bookshops, it could do a great deal of harm in the light of the implication. What follows is an acceptance of 'unintentional loose wording' and the pulping of the whole print run.

On the Record

One thing Gerald needed to remember was that his comments were always 'on the record'. Interviewers never turn off their metaphorical microphones. Gerald found this out the hard way. Interviewed for the Assemblies of God magazine *Redemption* in 1986, the interview went well. Relaxing at the end of the formal questions, Gerald appeared to imply in discussion that he was not sure of the inerrancy of Scripture. It was in the context of a relaxed discussion and Gerald was thinking aloud on a few issues. And it was a mouth-engaged-before-brain moment. The media storm that followed was a good lesson in making sure he stayed 'on record' and never assumed an interview was over! And just for the record, Gerald *does* believe in the inerrancy of Scripture.

The 1980s were full of Gerald Coates interviews in the Christian press. He was everywhere! It's his passion of course. The message has to get out there by every means possible. And magazines were keen for interviews, not least because Gerald was likely to say something controversial.

Even today, you can find plenty of websites taking a sideswipe at Gerald, using his comments out of context. But then when you read of who else the sites are criticising, you find he's in some pretty auspicious company!

Pioneer Network

With the demise of *Fulness* and its short-lived successor *Dovetail* magazine, Gerald wants to make sure that the churches he is relating to are kept informed of his thinking, plans and progress. *Pioneer Bulletin* is born. It is sent out free of charge (with a request for a 30p donation per copy) to any churches and individuals that want to hear from him. In the spring of 1983, its first edition, complete with a 'Pioneers and Settlers' article, is already talking about 'Pioneer Enterprises' as being a platform for Gerald's ministry.

By the winter of 1984, the wording has changed. No longer is it a bulletin 'for those who have a prayerful, caring interest' in Gerald's ministry. Now it's for 'a network of churches . . . linked through . . . team'. Welcome to Pioneer Network.

Gerald isn't alone in setting up a network. His good friend John Noble has Team Spirit up and running at about the same time. Stuart Bell is doing great things in the Lincolnshire area with his Ground Level team, and becomes a good friend to Gerald and Anona. Bryn Jones has started Harvestime (later Covenant Ministries) and Terry Virgo has Coastlands (later Newfrontiers). There are many more, including Roger Forster from Ichthus, who begins to work more closely with Gerald and John Noble.

Gerald's Pioneer group is more loosely defined than some. Without the structure of Ichthus and the stronger discipline of Harvestime, it attracts a broad group of churches, grateful for relationship and welcoming Gerald's teaching and prophetic ministry, without the feeling that they are being 'owned'.

Don't confuse lack of structure for lack of purpose though. Over the years, Pioneer has run (and continues to run) many courses, Bible weeks, leadership conferences, training sessions and more. One of the key successes has been in evangelism with the TIE Teams – Training In Evangelism. Teams of young people have been released onto the unsuspecting public in many towns and cities! Often they have prayed beforehand for specific contacts, seeing in the Spirit people they are going to meet and lives they are going to change.

Release

A successful home church. And a successful Pioneer movement. Something has to give though.

Gerald is travelling widely by now, leading the new Network. Although he has been released from regular preaching, he is still actually leading Cobham Christian Fellowship. But not that well. How can he when he is away so much? He isn't sure what to do. The phone call is from Gerald's old friend Peter Lyne.

'Gerald, can we meet? I feel God is saying something pretty big. And it's better we discuss it face to face than over the phone.'

They meet in a coffee shop in a hotel in Reading. Peter is looking serious.

'Gerald, I think it's about time that you gave up the leadership of the Cobham Fellowship and gave yourself to a wider, national ministry.'

Simple words. And a profound effect.

As Gerald drives home, he's not really aware of his surroundings. He feels almost dizzy. It's as if God by his Holy Spirit is right beside him. Peter's words have opened up a whole new set of thoughts for Gerald. As he prays through what has been discussed, Gerald is more and more certain that Peter is correct.

Maybe Gerald has been afraid to let go of the local in case the national doesn't work? Perhaps it's because he feels responsible for the Fellowship? But as the car journey home continues, Gerald sees things differently.

This is God's call and God's timing. He needs to step out in faith and trust that God will meet his needs. After all, if this is God's word for a new season, then God will also provide for all that is needed both financially and in terms of ministry.

Despite his lack of concentration on the driving, Gerald gets home without an accident. And with a clear sense that God has just opened a ministry door.

First Mike Blount, and later Martin Scott and Stuart Lindsell take over the Fellowship. It continues to grow, and the release that Gerald feels is palpable. Suddenly he can devote all his energies to the bigger national picture. And nothing comes much bigger than the March for Jesus.

11
KING OF THE NATIONS

'And finally,' Michael Buerk the newsreader looks towards the cameras, 'thousands of people with a Christian faith descended on London today. Marching from Hyde Park to Westminster, they joined around seven million people from one hundred and eighty nations in marching.'

Stunning figures.

This is the final 'Global March' in 2000. It is the culmination of years of passionate declarations on the streets of towns and cities, initially in the UK and then throughout the world.

The Start

Years earlier, when Gerald gets that first phone call from Roger Forster of Ichthus, he cannot have known what God is about to do. Together, they reach out to Lynn Green, the UK Director of Youth With A Mission, an evangelistic organisation, and the three begin to talk.

And talk . . . And talk . . .

The songwriter and worship leader Graham Kendrick has been pioneering Ichthus marches into Soho and other parts of

London and has, by this time, written a number of songs suitable for marching. Why not take this to the City of London? There is a perceived need to challenge the greed of the City, and an awareness of possible underhand practices.

So a date is set. On a rainy Saturday in May 1987, 5,000 people were expected – 15,000 turn up. Gerald and his friends are not even aware until the last minute of the actual numbers. Many have been sheltering under the arches of Smithfield Market, and it is only as the meeting begins and they step out into the rain that Gerald realises quite what an impact this event can have.

And it certainly has impact. Within a few weeks, insider dealing in the stock market is exposed. Then the stock market crashes. Gerald accepts this can be coincidence. But he is keenly aware that when Christians pray 'coincidences' tend to happen more frequently!

Such an amazing day needs repeating in Gerald's view. Lynn Green and his deputy Laurence Singlehurst are keen too. The concept has worked. Christians across the country have heard of the London march. Many have travelled long distances to be there. The effect on the City has been noted. Surely it is time for God's people to arise!

The problem is Roger has only planned to organise the one event. He has other plans for the year after. It could so easily have ended there. But the plans change, Roger comes on board, and March for Jesus becomes part of the vocabulary of thousands of churches in the UK and beyond. With a team chaired by Gerald's friend Steve Clifford and excellently managed by Erica Youngman Butler, the event grows and grows. The cry is to 'Make Way', to declare Christ on His throne, head of the church, Lord of the nations. A triumphalist message for sure. And one deeply rooted in prayer and the growing theology of the house church movement.

This is what Arthur Wallis had been teaching all those years ago. This is a church standing up to be counted. A church that is not willing to stay in the small hall at the end of the street. A church that has something to say. That speaks into the culture of the day. A church that reminds the nation it has been a mighty influence in earlier ages, and can be again.

Vast Numbers

Gerald is in his element. Organising, networking, speaking. The dates grow. The marches spread. The songs are sung in town centres. The prayers are shouted out on the city streets in London, Liverpool, Manchester, Birmingham, Bristol, Newcastle, Edinburgh, Glasgow, Cardiff, Brighton, and many more. Market towns such as Haywards Heath and Spalding. New towns such as Crawley, Peterborough, Stevenage and Milton Keynes. The Scottish highlands. The Scottish borders. Throughout Wales and Northern Ireland. Then overflowing to Ireland, the Continent, Paris, Berlin, Brussels, the United States, Canada, South America, Australia, New Zealand, Japan, Korea, India, enormous numbers in Africa.

How many take part? How many are affected by these declarations and prayers? What happens in the streets and cities? The full effect will only be seen in eternity, but with more than sixty million people marching over the years, in one hundred and eighty nations up to the last of the official marches in the year 2000, this is vast. And it's still going on. North and South America, in particular, have maintained their marches each year.

This is not a group of leaders trying to find a new way to mobilise the church. This is not a committee or a minister fraternal. This is friendship – a key fundamental of the house church movement. It's all because Gerald met up with Roger Forster, Lynn Green and Graham Kendrick.

Steve Clifford, part of Cobham Christian Fellowship at the time, and Director of March for Jesus, sees that the whole movement quickly became part of church culture in the UK:

'We were aware we were getting caught up in something so much bigger than any of its constituent parts.'

When you're talking of legacies, this is a hard one to beat.

Shout His Name

Shout His name! (clap x4) Jesus!
The highest name (clap x4) Jesus!
Shout a little louder!
(clap x4) Jesus!
I love that name
(clap 4x) Jesus!
We're gonna take that name
(clap 4x) Jesus!
To every nation
(clap 4x) Jesus!
Lift Him high!
(clap 4x) Jesus!
In this generation
King of the nations
Your kingdom come
In this generation
Your will be done
King of the nations
Your kingdom come
In this generation
Your will be done
I want to see your kingdom come

Extract taken from the song 'Shout His Name' by Graham

Young Gerald preaching, 1970

Tartar Road, Cobham, 1970

Nationwide Festival of Light, 1971

Gerald outside the Royal Albert Hall, 1977

Gerald interviewing Malcolm Muggeridge, 1980

Pioneer Team, 1984

Gerald, Lynn Green and Roger Forster, late eighties

Gerald in Masaka, Uganda with interpreter Robert Kayanja
(brother of John Sentamu, Archbishop of York), 1990

March for Jesus with Gerald, Roger Forster, Clive Calver,
John Noble and Anona, 1990

Gerald and Noel Richards, New Zealand, 1990

Jonathan, Anona, Gerald, Simon and Paul, early nineties

Gerald with David Yonggi Cho, Wembley Arena, 1994

Gerald, March for Jesus, Trafalgar Square, 1995

Cliff Richard, King Michael and Queen Anne of Romania,
Gerald and Anona, Cliff's house, 1995

Gerald with John Arnott, Toronto, mid-nineties

Emmanuel Centre, Marsham Street, London, 1997

Gerald interviewing on the main stage
Wembley Stadium, 1997

Gerald and R. T. Kendall, 1998

Gerald with Lyndon Bowring, Rob Parsons and Steve Chalke
March for Jesus, 1999

Nathan Ramsden (adopted son), 2000

Gerald with Bill Johnson, 2008

Luke (adopted son) who lived in Coates Road, 2009

Kendrick. Copyright ©1992 Make Way Music

Just one of the many shouted declarations on the streets. Led by Noel Richards and Graham Kendrick, and accompanied by Graham's songs such as 'Let the Flame Burn Brighter', 'Shine Jesus Shine' and 'Meekness and Majesty', the crowds sing and shout through the streets, banners and balloons to the fore, giving leaflets out, making Christian declarations in front of the Town Halls up and down the country.

And churches working together. There's a miracle right there. Churches in the same towns that hardly speak to each other are suddenly standing side by side. This is theology right there on the streets. Relationships that work. And Christ's kingdom declared. What has been rediscovered in the house church movement finds its voice in the March for Jesus movement.

Wembley

'Are you sure about this Noel?' Gerald is on the phone to Noel Richards. 'Taking the whole of Wembley stadium for one big event?'

Noel laughs. A little nervously perhaps.

It's the mid-nineties and by now the church landscape in the UK has been radically changed. There are thousands of house churches, many streams and movements. Most of the churches are far too big for houses now. They are buying their own warehouses, redeveloping closed cinemas and more.

And those churches remaining in the older denominations are different too. The Pentecostal movement has thawed out in their icy relationship with the new kids on the block. Many Baptist churches have become charismatic, accepting that the gifts of the Holy Spirit are for today. Methodist churches too.

And the Anglicans. Pioneered in the early days by such people as Michael Harper and David Watson, the evangelical wing of the

Church of England has grown in importance. Key centres have broken through their formality into a new freedom in worship – Holy Trinity, Brompton and St Andrews, Chorleywood in the lead.

At a time when churches and denominations have not even been speaking to each other, let alone trying to work together, the momentum and communication developed in March for Jesus has to go somewhere. And that somewhere is Wembley.

This is a time when Queen's 'We Are the Champions' is being sung from the terraces of football grounds up and down the country. Gerald and Noel feel it is time to fill stadiums with a different song. The event is to be called 'Champion of the World'. A time of worship, praying and declaration, very much in the mould of the March for Jesus, it quickly builds up momentum.

Noel and Tricia are busy writing material. Noel is keen to see Christ as the Champion of the World, replacing the chants of the football terraces with powerful declaration from thousands of believers. He and Tricia write 'Champion' to try and capture the moment:

The world is looking for a hero
We know the greatest One of all.
The mighty Ruler of the nations
King of kings and Lord of lords.
Who took the nature of a servant
And gave His life to save us all.

We will raise a shout
We will shout it out
He is the champion
Of the world.
We will raise a shout
We will shout it out

He is the champion
Of the world

Extract taken from the song 'Champion' by Noel & Tricia Richards. Copyright ©1994 Thankyou Music*

The lead up to the day itself has seen torrential rain, but on the day, the rain stops. There is a lot of prayer on that point!

Gerald and Noel are there early. The people start to arrive. More and more. Thousands upon thousands.

On one day in June 1997, 43,000 people gather at Wembley Stadium. The Christian band Delirious? play, along with Graham Kendrick, Dave Bilbrough and many more. There is an honouring of the worship songwriters and as Noel leads in worship, all 43,000 call on God asking Him to move in revival.

It's an amazing day. There is a tangible sense of the presence of the Holy Spirit on the gathering. Reflecting the victorious theology of the house church movement, Noel Richards declares that this could be 'the last great breath of God' before Christ's return.

One attendee that day is an old man from the Western Isles of Scotland who was one of the boys that helped in the last great revival on British shores in the Hebrides (1949–52). As Gerald interviews him, there is a rise of faith that God can do the same again.

Only in eternity will we know the full force of such events on the climate of our nation, but once again, the churches had gathered with one voice and with one agenda. And, once again, the impetus has been from the new churches with their triumphalist rallying cry to the nation.

Calling All Nations

Noel has for many years dreamed of filling football stadiums with praising Christians. As far back as 1986, in the wake of the Live

Aid concert the year before, Noel has begun to see the possibility. Why not Christians instead of music fans? Why not Christian groups instead of secular bands?

The success of Wembley in 1997 leads to an even greater venture. Europe is seen at this time as something of an evangelist's graveyard from a UK point of view. But the continent is opening up after the fall of the Iron Curtain and the literal removal of the Berlin wall.

It's 5 a.m. in a Berlin hotel room. Gerald is awake. Skipping breakfast, he stays in his room and prays: 'Lord, this feels really big. I need your help today. Please Lord, use this event to begin to open up Europe to your gospel. Use me, Lord.'

Gerald remembers some of the prophetic words over his life. This is God's work, not his.

Berlin is the focal point for this Calling All Nations event, in July 2006. As Gerald arrives at the stadium, he's grateful for good weather. And he's not alone – 22,000 people from more than thirty nations also gather to declare Jesus as Lord. As Noel begins to leads the worship, the songs are beamed out by a number of Christian television channels. Delirious? perform. Graham Kendrick is there, as are Godfrey Birtill, Matt Redman, Paul Oakley, Ruben Morgan, Sue Rinaldi, Tim Hughes, Y Friday, Chris Bowater and Dave Bilbrough. A veritable who's who of the UK Christian worship scene at the time. Gerald speaks on that day. And many listen. The house church movement of the 1970s and 80s is finding a new expression, not just in the UK, but throughout Europe.

And Gerald's ministry is growing. Invitations from practically every European country flood in after the Calling All Nations event. From five people in a house church to nations gathering – God's sense of humour in taking a postman and window dresser into a place of power, and in mixing with people in high places too.

Cliff

Gerald is occasionally accused of referencing his friends in high places. But the fact is there *are* friends in high places! One of the most notable is Cliff Richard.

Gerald and Cliff first meet at a concert sometime around 1978, where both are guests of someone else. A conversation follows, when the two realise they are close neighbours. Cliff doesn't need friends in the sense of new people to meet and spend time with. But he does need friends he can confide in and pray with. And in this small-statured pastor with a large personality, Cliff feels he has found someone who can help him. As Cliff himself puts it, Gerald has a 'no frills' honesty which Cliff finds refreshing. Perhaps unusual too, in the celebrity world Cliff inhabits. Gerald is able to keep a confidence and at the same time is not over-awed by celebrity culture. A friend and a pastor rolled into one.

Over the months that follow, the friendship builds. As much as possible, Cliff makes Cobham Christian Fellowship his home. Usually, he turns up just as the meeting begins in order not to bring attention to himself. So much so that one time, a visitor complains that they have to sit next to a 'Cliff Richard look-alike'!

As well as Cliff performing at Kingdom Life Bible week and similar endeavours, when he can, Cliff, along with his manager Bill Latham, attends Gerald and Anona's New Year bashes. Through Gerald, Cliff gets to know Shelia Walsh well and, as a result, singing collaborations and tours follow.

Post Bag

Cliff Richard gets a phenomenal post bag each week, the majority of it fan mail. But interspersed with the fan letters are pleas for help, people asking about Cliff's Christian faith and seeking guidance. Cliff has felt unable to deal with these and it is through his friendship with Gerald that he is able to decide what to do.

Gerald sets up administration within the church in order to answer them, offering spiritual guidance to those writing.

Gerald is a call-to point for prayer as well, on one occasion taking a well-known Christian healer with him to pray for Cliff's back. The results are immediate.

Cliff clearly enjoys Gerald's company, as witnessed by watching movies together – Cliff is in tears as they watch Mel Gibson's *The Passion of the Christ* – and they share many meals together. But when asked to recall moments in their relationship, it's not tears that come to mind. Cliff thinks first of the times of laughter.

On one occasion, Gerald and Anona are Cliff's guests at a restaurant on New Year's Eve. As midnight approaches, Cliff asks Gerald what they should do. Gerald stands and raises his glass. 'Ladies and gentlemen, to the King and his Kingdom!'

Cliff's guests stand and repeat the refrain. Then, to the amazement of Cliff's party, the whole restaurant – full of the rich and powerful – stand together and repeat the toast. Do they know what they are saying? Probably not. But at one moment in time, God breaks in, in an amazing and somewhat humorous way!

Rick

Rick Parfitt of Status Quo is also a friend of Gerald. Gerald, who got to know Rick through a mutual friend in the Moody Blues, is there for the most tragic moment in Rick's life.

One morning, Gerald gets a call from Marietta, Rick's wife. Can he and Anona come over to the house straight away? There's been a tragedy. Their daughter Heidi, who plays with Gerald and Anona's youngest boy, has fallen into the swimming pool and drowned. Rick thought she had been with Marietta; Marietta thought she was with Rick.

As Gerald and Anona make the short trip to Guildford, they pray. Gerald recalls it as feeling like one of the longest drives of his life. When they arrive, they find Rick curled up in the corner of the hallway, tears streaming down his face. By now family have arrived, but Rick and Marietta need the spiritual help Gerald and Anona can offer.

Gerald and Rick read scripture together. Sitting together in the corner of the hallway, they seek out the comfort that comes from God's words of life – words of life in a moment of tragedy.

Boy George

Gerald is used by God in some surprising ways. None more so than when he writes to singer Boy George.

Boy George has been interviewed by *The Guardian*. In the interview, he explains that he has become a godfather and goes on to describe the baby's christening. He explains in the article how dull the service was, expressing that he feels it should have been a moment of celebration. There should have been a party!

Gerald is impressed by what he says and writes to Boy George to thank him for the article. One of the members of his band is a Christian and observes the effect on Boy George as he reads the letter. It turns out that sadly, a number of so-called Christians have also written to Boy George, expressing in strong language, their views that because of his lifestyle he has no right to be a godfather to any child. In contrast, Gerald's letter is a delight and surprise to Boy George.

Move on a couple of years, and the same band member has invited Gerald and Anona to a concert. To the surprise of all, part way through the concert, Boy George announces, 'We have someone really big in Christianity with us tonight.'

He goes on to dedicate the next two songs to Gerald and Anona, singing versions of 'This Little Light of Mine' and 'Down by the Riverside'. After the concert, Gerald and Anona are invited onto the gleaming and giant tour bus. There, they spend an hour or two talking with Boy George.

At one point, one of the organisers comes into the tour bus to remind Boy George that some fans are still waiting for him.

'But I'm with my friends Gerald and Anona! They'll just have to wait!'

Words of life in surprising settings. All because of a letter.

Alvin

It is through Cliff that Alvin Stardust comes into Gerald and Anona's lives. Cliff brings him along to a church event. Alvin has been to church before, but nothing quite like this. A few of the others in the congregation notice he is there – hard to miss with his trademark sideburns and swept-back hair. What they may also have noticed is his increasing nervousness as the preach goes on.

Is this for him? Has the preacher prepared a special talk just for him? It feels that way. As Gerald speaks, every word lands in an open heart.

At the end of the sermon, there is an invitation to respond, to accept Christ as Lord and Saviour. One of the first hands raised that night is that of the pop star. A special moment and one that profoundly changes Alvin Stardust for the rest of his life. He goes through many problems in years to come but never loses his faith. At his premature death from cancer in 2014, he is recorded in the many obituaries as a godly man and one of the kindest people in the pop industry.

As the TV news item shows a final picture of the coffin, as the service ends, Gerald reflects, not for the first time, on how God has been able to use his words, and make of them words of life.

12
WORDS OF LIFE

If you talk to Gerald, he's cautious about using the word 'leader' or 'apostle' regarding his ministry. There is no such hesitation when you start to refer to him as a 'prophet'.

This is not a hair-suited Old Testament prophet, though, but a well-dressed, bespectacled, slightly tubby, twenty-first century variety. (And when he started out, it was more like a twentieth-century bright purple-suited variety!)

Prophecy is key to Gerald. Both that received for his life and that given to others. Words of life, acted upon and life changing.

The idea that God can speak outside of the words of the Bible is revisited in the early days of the house church movement. Along with an awareness that God has not finished with 'apostles', there is the awareness that 'prophets' still exist and can speak God's words into people's lives, both individually and corporately. Such prophetic words can never carry the weight of Scripture and, as the Bible encourages us, they need to be weighed and considered. But prophetic words are alive and well in the twenty-first-century church, and occasionally the description goes beyond someone who brings a prophetic word, to defining someone as a prophet.

Gerald is careful how he says things, but there is no doubt he believes he hears God regularly on both local and national issues. But before we get carried away with what Gerald has and hasn't said (and the internet is pretty full of that), let's look at prophetic words that have been brought into Gerald and Anona's lives and how such words have shaped them.

A high value is placed on the prophetic within the house church movement generally, and many of the different house church streams have moved forward and changed the way they work on the basis of a prophetic word. After all, if this is God speaking, the church needs to listen and respond.

Gerald finds himself listening particularly closely to some prophetic words back in 1990.

Dale and Jean Gentry

Returning from a conference in the north of England, Gerald is tired. He drives his Brooklands Green Ford Capri through the gates of Clive House, and is met by an excited Anona.

'You'd better sit down for this one!'

Mug of tea in hand, Gerald catches up on what has been happening. Dale and Jean Gentry are prophetic preachers from an Assemblies of God background, based in Texas, and have been speaking into the different Pioneer churches. None more so than Cobham Christian Fellowship.

As Dale speaks at Cobham, he feels a strong word from God for them. There is a large turnout, filling the hired hall.

'Thousands are going to become Christians in this area, and it's going to happen quickly. But you are in the wrong place. Your dreams are too small. Cobham Christian Fellowship needs to die to its dreams and begin to pick up on the bigger calling God has for you.'

'You will be influential to many and touch the lives of the

influential. You will touch London with your ministry. God is going to give you a new boldness. And a new hall to work from. And Gerald needs a father. He needs a father figure working with him for all God is going to do.'

As Gerald listens to the words as Anona remembers them, his mug of tea remains untouched. There is much that is new for him, but much that he feels God has been speaking about already. Especially a new hall to meet in, and in touching the influential. Gerald feels that reaching the influential and the word about London are related. Somehow God is going to open a door for Pioneer right into the centre of London.

The tiredness from the journey is gone.

Later, lying in bed, sleep doesn't come. Gerald's mind is whirring. He's so grateful to God for such moments. Unable on his own, even with a prophetic gift, to identify all God is saying, prophecies such as this are essential. He knows the Gentrys well. He trusts their God-given gift of prophecy. It fits with a number of things Gerald feels God has been saying when he's been studying the Bible. That God would use him in such a way! Amazing! There's a torrent of praise and of tongues speaking as Gerald eventually falls asleep.

The next morning, Gerald's mind is at work, identifying as much as he can with what is meant by the different parts of the prophecy. Especially what to make of the father figure? There is only one father to Gerald, as far as he is concerned. Although many have spoken into Gerald's life over the years, only one can be considered a father to him; only one has consistently supported and helped direct Gerald's growing ministry.

John Noble

Later that day, Gerald is on the phone to John Noble. How are they to interpret the word? John certainly doesn't dismiss it. He is open to the prophetic prompting.

Months later at a conference at Holy Trinity Brompton, John Noble shares from the microphone, with tears running down his face, how God has intervened and how as a result of the prophetic word, he and Christine are moving to Surrey from East London.

This is a significant move. And a sacrificial one for John and Christine. They have their own network of churches and strong connections to the Romford area. But God has spoken. John knows it is His voice, and they move to be with Gerald and Anona. Gerald has his father figure. Although much that follows in Gerald's ministry is an outworking of Gerald's giftings and calling, behind him is the substantial spiritual figure that is John Noble.

Paul Cain

1990 is a significant year for Gerald. Not only has the church received key prophetic words from the Gentrys, but Gerald finds himself at a John Wimber conference, alongside the recognised prophet Paul Cain.

Something needs to be said here. Many reading these words will be aware of Paul's recorded 'fall from grace' and his own admission of having to deal with various temptations, primarily the temptations of homosexuality and alcoholism. Many may also be aware that he has resumed ministry in recent times. Some, Gerald among them, are not so sure of the extent of the 'fall', believing it is more temptation than action. Whatever the facts, there is no doubt that Paul Cain's ministry has been one of the most accurate prophetic ministries in a generation. And his words at the John Wimber conference appear to have been particularly clear.

John Wimber, a larger than life American with an apostolic and healing ministry, has invited Paul Cain to speak alongside him at the London conference. John invites Gerald to join him for a meal.

'Excuse me,' a young American man leans over John and Gerald as they are eating. 'Do you have a son called Jonathan?'

'Er, yes. Yes I do.' Gerald isn't sure what this is about.

'You see, I'm with Paul Cain across the room there.' He points to another table. 'Paul felt to tell you that God is going to use your son in a significant way.'

It's not often Gerald is speechless! It transpires that there is much more to the prophetic word than that. The word, later explained in full by Paul Cain, revolves around 'Nathan, Jonathan and Nations'.

As Gerald stands in the meeting later, Paul Cain again points to him.

'You are a man with a coat. No, a man called Coat. Is that right?'

'It's Coates. Gerald Coates.'

'Yes. I see crowds marching. You are leading. I see you as a controversial figure. Is that right?'

Laughter from the rest of the congregation. Gerald, the outspoken house church leader is in a congregation made up mainly of Anglicans; people he has spent years criticising.

'It's the nations. Marching for the nations. With Nathan. Jonathan too. Your adopted and your own sons.'

After the meeting, Paul gives Gerald a card with the information on it. It's what Paul has heard from God long before he has even met Gerald, written on a card as a reminder, before the meeting. The card confirms all that Paul has said publicly. And against the word 'Family' is the word 'Adopted???' Three question marks follow the word.

Nathan

Paul Cain has no idea as to the accuracy of his words. Not only seeing the March for Jesus, by then well underway as an annual event, but Gerald's son Jonathan – and Nathan.

Gerald is in a youth meeting earlier in the year. He points to Nathan and prophesies over him, saying that someday he and Gerald will work together, and as proof of that, God is telling Gerald that Nathan has had a supernatural birth, something Nathan is not aware of.

Nathan returns home and relays this to his mother. The words are such a shock to her, she falls to the floor, influenced by the Holy Spirit. What Nathan doesn't know is that he had indeed been a miracle baby. The doctors thought he had been born brain-damaged due to complications, but with prayer from his parents, he pulled through without any damage whatsoever.

Linda, Nathan's mum, writes to Gerald to tell him this and to ask that he 'supernaturally adopt' Nathan alongside Nathan's own parents:

'As Hannah gave Samuel to Eli, so we want to give Nathan to you. We don't know how this is to work. No doubt you have thoughts on this. What we want you to know is that we freely give Nathan to you to prepare for the ministry of the gospel and all that will entail.'

Paul Cain's prophecy has added confirmation at a crucial time. Nathan is being prepared in a supernatural way, just as he has been born in a supernatural way.

Anona

'Adopted?' And three question marks.

Anona ponders Paul Cain's words. Why the strong emphasis? Why write the question mark more than once if it is just for Nathan? The phone call answers the question. It is a call that changes Anona's life.

Anona's just been out with her mum. It's a weekly thing. Every Tuesday afternoon. A visit to the shops or a garden centre and then a cup of tea and a chat. This time, they've called in on

Amanda for the cup of tea.

Anona's back home at Clive House, in the large kitchen, sorting out a casserole for tea. It's just gone in the oven when the phone call from Amanda comes through.

'Anona. I don't know quite how to say this, but your mum – she's not your mother. That woman is *not* your mother!'

'What are you talking about Amanda? I don't understand.'

'She can't be! She's nothing like you.'

'I know that. She's small and darker. But that's no reason to say she's not my mum!'

'But it's more than that Anona. It's not just appearance. There's *nothing* similar about you!'

The casserole is forgotten and burning at the edges. Gerald finds Anona in the darkened kitchen, sitting quietly, trying to take in all she has heard. Amanda is very perceptive and has some professional knowledge of family traits and likenesses. And, to be honest, Anona has always suspected something. She has always felt the outsider in the family.

And it helps clear up one other thing too. Her father had abused her. Emotionally, physically and sexually. She hates to think of it. But if he is not her actual father, that starts to make a bit more sense.

In the darkened kitchen, as evening brings in its shadows, Anona relives the pain of those early years. Her father entering her bedroom, throwing back the blankets from her bed as she sleeps . . . Anona shudders. Tears begin to fall. She's received ministry for these things, of course she has. But the phone call brings it all back, as if it were yesterday.

By the time Gerald arrives, the tears have stopped, but Anona feels glued to her kitchen stool, unable to move. As Gerald holds her in his arms, she cries again. Tears of relief as much as anything. Relief that after all, he isn't her father.

The phone call begins two years of investigations. Birth certificates. Church records. The Family Records Centre. And an adoption certificate.

There's a sudden sense of freedom from her adoptive father's cruelty. A release from believing the lies he used to tell: that she was stupid, ugly and no use to anyone. A release from the literal hurts and bruises. And release from the sexual abuse. All prayed for many years before. But with the realisation of her adoption, Anona feels finally free, released. A new life – at the age of forty-three!

Her real mother is found. Christine Jones. Formerly a shorthand typist. Retired and living in Cheshire. A whirlwind wartime romance had left her pregnant and in need of a family to adopt the baby.

That wasn't all. Better than a detective novel, Anona finds out from Christine that the father is not British, nor one of the many American servicemen, but German.

A Faded Pink File

Trying to find her father will be harder.

Allowed out of the prisoner of war camp during the day, Werner had met up with Christine. After the war, he'd returned to Germany.

Eventually, the original adoption correspondence is found. Still held in council records, Anona is handed a faded pink file. Photographs. Letters. Requests for adoption.

There are tears as she reads it.

But no clues as to how to find the father.

Letters to the International Red Cross and the British Embassy in Germany produce results though.

Two years after the research begins, Gerald and Anona fly to Germany. In Dortmund, father and daughter meet for the first time.

With new families in Cheshire and Dortmund, there is a lot of catching up to do. And, later still, Anona tells the whole story in her book *I Wish I Was*. It's well worth reading. From rejection to redemption. And a God who cares about us enough to prompt a phone call on a Tuesday evening after a cup of tea.

The Jigsaw

There's one other prophecy for Gerald that's worth mentioning before we leave this chapter.

Cleland Thom is a lively figure from the Pentecostal movement. On one occasion, he picks Gerald out from a meeting and brings a word that has stayed with Gerald throughout his ministry.

'I see you doing a jigsaw and getting very frustrated with it. You are so keen to complete it, but can't find the right pieces. This is what God says: "You don't have all the pieces! I'm calling you to work with others to fulfil your calling on your life." This is not a one-man operation; this is a call to work together.'

Gerald takes the word seriously. His methodology has always been to work with others where he can, but this particular prophecy makes him even more intentional. His desire is to bless others, to see leaders released, and for them to know what God is saying for their own lives.

So, from prophecies for Gerald, to those Gerald has brought to others with some far-reaching results . . .

13

THE PROPHET

There's a website called 'Deception in the Church', and it starts like this:

'Great deception is afoot in the churches today, happening right before our very eyes. In fact, it may have already come to your church. False doctrines, a different gospel, and even doctrines of demons have been introduced into many churches via books, music, videos, teachers and movements that claim to be of God.'

It's not the only site like this. There are a few around. And it's fairly typical in what it says of Gerald's prophecies. It cites two in particular – one to R.T. Kendall and one relating to an earthquake in New Zealand – and declares that Gerald is a false prophet because what he said didn't happen.

More of that in a moment, but first things first. Gerald is in good company. The same site announces that a number of other leading men and women in the church are just as false, including people like Reinhard Bonnke, Jack Hayford, David Yonggi Cho and pretty much anyone linked with the 'Toronto Blessing'. Some of the world's leading church builders, teachers and authors get a mention. Another site called 'Christian Witness' sets out pretty

:h the same points and adds a few others they wish to criticise, including Nicky Gumbel (and the Alpha Course), John Wimber and Terry Virgo.

These sites and others like them seem to have a single agenda – to pull down anything that isn't in line with some very narrow, dubious theology. Just so you know.

We'll have a look at the prophecies that are questioned, but let's start out with Gerald's journey.

The Laboratory

We go back to those early meetings of the Fabulous Fourteen to get a sense of the birth of a gift in the prophetic. The meetings act as a kind of laboratory for prophetic words. Gerald is particularly influenced by David Mansell, someone with a very clear prophetic gift and an ability to speak into situations and transform them with a prophetic word.

All this is new to Gerald at the time. He's been baptised in the Holy Spirit and is developing his understanding of speaking in tongues, but beyond that, there isn't much going on until those meetings.

At those first meetings, most of the Fabulous Fourteen are discussing the role of the apostle. Both the fact that it still operates today and that many of them around the table are, to a greater or lesser extent, already exercising apostolic gifts in the way they are leading.

Gerald feels he isn't part of this particular discussion. But as soon as the conversation turns to the equally new idea (at the time) that there are such things as modern-day prophets, Gerald gets animated.

Early prophetic attempts are along the lines of speaking as if God is speaking. Kind of a 'Thus says the Lord' type of prophecy, though Gerald always avoids the King James Bible language! But

Gerald soon learns that this is not always the best way to bring God's words to someone. It doesn't need the supposed authority of God 'speaking' it. Gerald has observed too many of these seemingly authoritative words that don't actually say much. 'Thus says the Lord: "I love you".'

Over a period of time, Gerald develops more of a conversational approach. 'I feel God may be saying . . .' or 'If God were to speak to you right now, he might be saying this . . .' And so on.

We can see some of Gerald's early thinking on the prophetic in articles he writes. In *Fulness* magazine, Gerald writes of 'living in the prophetic' – the need to be a prophetic people, to be authentic and to ensure there is no credibility gap. Gerald is human. He makes mistakes. But he also tries to live what he preaches. This gives him the authority to prophesy and speak into other people's lives.

In these early days, Gerald's on a journey in his public ministry – and doesn't always get it right. Like the time he feels God say that a young man's name is Mark. Gerald is on the stage and doesn't want to be embarrassed, so he keeps silent. Instead he asks the young man his name. It's Mark!

Move on one meeting and again Gerald feels there will be a 'Mark' in the meeting that he is meant to bring a prophetic word for. This time he feels that this 'Mark' will be sitting in a certain block in the room. So he draws a picture of the seating and puts the word 'Mark' next to the block in question. During the meeting, Gerald says, 'There's someone called Mark in the meeting tonight. I want you to stand.'

Only one person stands. He's in the block Gerald has drawn. Mark comes to the front. Gerald shows him the hand-drawn map. The rise in faith in the meeting is palpable.

Over the years Gerald has felt God has spoken to him and through him many times. Sometimes a gentle word for an individual. Sometimes a strong word for a nation. And many times accompanied by vivid pictures of what Gerald believes God is showing him.

Scorched Earth

It's early 2002. Gerald is sitting with his Reformed pastor friend R.T. Kendall in his office at Westminster Chapel. R.T. has just announced his retirement and is planning his return to the US. It's a casual conversation.

'So what do you see happening next, Gerald?'

R.T. is asking in connection with the UK church and where Gerald sees it going. Gerald's reaction is surprising.

Suddenly Gerald is gasping for breath, tears streaming down his face. With deep sobbing, he replies:

'I see a scorched earth. I see a scorched earth!'

It's a military phrase and has been used at this time by the Taliban and Al Qaeda in connection with their attacks on the West, and in particular the attacks on the United States the previous year, on 11 September 2001.

As Gerald sits in R.T.'s study, he vividly sees parts of the UK in green and other parts in brown. The UK is going to be under attack. What will it look like? Gerald doesn't know. But he feels, at that moment, something of the heart of God for this nation. And sees for a moment in time what is coming.

Possibly Gerald sees it as a spiritual attack, but as we now know, the London bombings in 2005 highlighted a literal 'scorched earth' attack from Al Qaeda, both in the bombings on 7 July and the second attempted bombings on 21 July that year.

On 21 July 2005, Gerald gets an early warning of that second attack. One of his friends in Pioneer is part of the response team for any London attacks, and Gerald receives a phone call from him asking for prayer for what at first appears to be a chemical attack on the Underground. One of the results of both the vision and the phone call has been Gerald setting up an emergency prayer network across the churches of the UK.

Heathrow

Gerald has been praying. He senses God is telling him of another potential terrorist incident at Heathrow airport. But who should he tell? If he goes to the police and announces that God has told him, he will be laughed out of the station doors.

Gerald remembers that there is someone in one of Peter Lyne's churches who is high up in airport management. Peter puts them in touch. The man has just moved back to Heathrow.

Gerald shares his word from God. It's taken seriously.

'Thank you Gerald. Thank you. Leave it with me.'

Gerald doesn't know the results of the security discussions, of course. But at a meeting some months later, the pastor of the Heathrow manager is there and introduces Gerald to someone as 'one of the most prophetic guys in the country'.

Personal and Public

On occasion, Gerald has given words for individuals publicly. But many prophetic words Gerald has had over the years have been personal and delivered personally.

Like the time Gerald tells a surprised Joel Edwards that he will be the next General Director of the Evangelical Alliance. No one has ever been promoted from within the Evangelical Alliance to the senior post, so Joel simply doesn't believe Gerald. He thinks he is joking. But it happens.

Or the time Gerald tells journalist John Buckeridge not to 'give it all away', but to stay on board with the new owners of *Christianity* magazine. He does and is now Deputy Chief Executive of Premier Radio, which includes oversight of all the magazines. John keeps a copy of Gerald's prophecy with him as a reminder of God's faithfulness.

Another time, Gerald is speaking on changing from being a Saul to a David, picking up on the story in 1 Samuel in the Bible. At the end he calls forward a young man who has been playing in the band.

'What is your name?'

'My name is Aaron.'

'What is your middle name?'

'My middle name is Saul.'

Cheers from the congregation. The young man changes his middle name by Deed Poll to David and today he is a successful musician.

From Canterbury to Canada

Gerald is in Canterbury for a series of meetings when he sees a young man from the university. Gerald speaks to him prophetically – words that clearly have an impact.

Ten years later, Gerald is preaching at Holy Trinity Brompton. He points to a man in the congregation.

'God says to you that He has put something on your heart. It hasn't happened yet. But it will do. Be patient! It will happen!'

The man introduces himself to Gerald after the meeting. He's the same person Gerald spoke prophetically to all those years ago – words that have sustained him. And now God has spoken again. More sustaining words. More words of encouragement. He knows exactly what the prophetic words mean and he intends to hold on to them.

His name is Stuart Hazeldine. And he held on to the words. Today he is a successful film director. He was shortlisted as 'Outstanding Debut by a British Writer, Director or Producer' at the BAFTA awards for one of his early films, and is currently involved in bringing two new films to conclusion. One is *Paradise Lost*, based on Milton's poem and the other is *The Shack*.

The Shack is a very successful Christian work of fiction, where a grieving parent is invited to meet with God at 'the shack'. Having been filmed in Los Angeles, this multi-million-pound screen version is being edited in Vancouver, Canada – a long way from that first prophetic word in Canterbury.

Difficult Moments

Sometimes the word Gerald gets puts him in a difficult position. Like the time he interprets a picture at a conference. He shares it privately with one of the leaders.

In an earlier session, someone has shared publicly a picture of an oak tree. An invisible axe has felled it. But out of the stump, several trees grow. There has been no interpretation of the picture in the meeting at the time.

Gerald shares with the leader that he thinks it is about a main leader being removed but that this would facilitate new leaders coming through.

The next thing Gerald knows, the leader Gerald has shared it with is at the microphone, saying Gerald has an interpretation to the earlier picture and is now going to explain it. As Gerald shares what he feels is the interpretation, he is acutely aware that the leader of one of the early charismatic Anglican groups is behind him on the stage. This could be something that relates to him. Gerald is on the spot. This is embarrassing.

And it proves so. The man leaves before the meeting is finished. He does not attend any further meetings or conferences with that particular group.

There's difficult and there's funny. Like the time Gerald is on stage, sharing another picture.

It's a picture of an octopus over London. It is about reaching out over the city with the gospel. But as Gerald shares, he's very aware that he has lost his audience. There's giggling, shuffling in the seats.

He leans forward to one of the leaders on the front row.

'What has happened?' he asks, 'What have I said?'

'Well,' says the leader, 'I think you meant to say "tentacles".'

Spring Harvest

It's April 1995 at the Spring Harvest Easter event. Gerald has a sense that God will use him particularly this evening. It's no surprise to him that later in the meeting he has three clear words of prophecy for three different individuals.

The first is well-known Christian publisher, Peter Meadows. The founding editor of *Buzz* and a co-founder of Spring Harvest, he is at that time also the editor of *Christianity* magazine.

Peter is called to the front of the meeting. With microphone in hand, Gerald begins to speak.

'You have been trying to slip into the shadows, but God is calling you into the light. Seven years ago you had an idea. The time was not right. But now is the time. This is the time to do what is on your heart.'

Accurate? It certainly was. Peter had been working with Mission to London in 1984 with the evangelist Luis Palau and had been frustrated by the lack of impact on the city as a whole. Over the years that followed, he had begun to dream. Seven years previously, he had worked up new proposals for a Christian radio station, but was thwarted by the regulations then in force.

Gerald doesn't know as he speaks that night that the regulations regarding radio are in the process of changing. Applications have been made, but despite his obvious production abilities, Peter Meadows intends to step back. He responds to the prophetic word that night, and taking the helm, Premier Radio, the UK's leading Christian radio station, now broadcasting to more than 500,000 people a week, is born.

The second person on the platform that night is the wife of a prominent leader of a large Christian organisation. Gerald speaks publicly as to what he feels God is going to do with the two of them and where he feels God will be sending them in the world.

It is completely accurate. So much so that as the word is spoken over the wife that night, she is unable to physically move afterwards. God has rooted her to the spot as His Spirit ministers to her. What Gerald doesn't know is that conversations were already taking place between the husband and wife regarding their call to a certain nation. As this is being written, they are in place, in the country Gerald felt God was leading them to, and are involved in reaching key people across that nation. Because of the nation involved, this book cannot give any more details, but suffice to say, the prophetic word is spot on.

Intriguingly, her father-in-law had worked in this country before his son was born, and had been praying for the couple to work there too. He had never told them. They had not been aware of it. But God was.

The Word to R.T. Kendall

So here's one of the prophetic words from Gerald that has got him into trouble with the 'false prophet' brigade. It's the third word from the platform that night at Spring Harvest:

'I wonder, Dr Kendall, if you could come here please. God has put such a deep concern (on you) . . . for Westminster. Not just the Chapel but for all of those that live in it – within its shadow. I see that God has narrowed you down and narrowed you down and narrowed you down and the cry has gone up (from you) . . . "How long, how long, how long?" . . . The Spirit of the Lord is upon you. The Spirit of the Lord will come upon you in increasing power, but you need to understand that over these next eighteen months, although many attacks will come, if you are faithful to God, faithful to all that He's taught you, and faithful to your brothers, not seeking to achieve in human strength what only God can achieve by His Holy Spirit, in eighteen months from this month, in eighteen months from April 1995, your church, Westminster Chapel, will be unrecognisable – completely, utterly and totally unrecognisable.'

Gerald goes on to talk about people in the street responding to the Good News and praying:

'And it will come from the most unlikely sources – it will not come through the people you would like it to be through, it'll come through the most unlikely sources. And if you keep your heart and your eyes open, the Spirit of God is going to surprise us all. The Spirit of God is going to surprise us all.'

There it is.

Did it happen? It depends of course as to how you interpret the words. Detractors would say that nothing happened. There was no revival. But R.T. underwent a personal revival, and there is no doubt that his increased networking beyond the boundaries that a pastor of a Reformed church would normally have, produced a great deal of fruit from 'unlikely sources'. Gerald has a card from R.T. on which is written, 'A day never to be forgotten', referring to one of the meetings R.T. and Gerald co-hosted at that time.

Some church members left during this time. This was primarily because of links to another unlikely source – the Toronto Blessing (more of that later). Gerald recalls the head of the Fellowship of Evangelical Churches complaining that the Chapel was changing out of all recognition – exactly what Gerald had prophesied. It was meant as a complaint, but Gerald takes it as a confirmation the prophecy has been correct.

R.T. says that God did indeed move powerfully during that eighteen-month period. Near the end of that time, Gerald gets an invitation to speak at the Chapel. When he arrives, the worship has already started. There are bodies all over the floor as the Holy Spirit ministers. Gerald is shocked to say the least.

'I wanted to surprise you,' says R.T.

What about the bit relating to people in the streets of Westminster responding? It wasn't around Westminster Chapel, but it did happen in Westminster. On the evening of 5 September 1997, Gerald drives slowly through the City of Westminster. The slowness is forced. There are thousands on the streets, preparing to sleep out overnight for the funeral of Princess Diana the next day. One is a Christian lady from a Pioneer church. As midnight approaches, another lady stands up and invites others to stand and pray.

'God, I don't even know if you exist,' she says, 'but all I do know is that this nation needs you right now.'

People on the streets. Praying. Perhaps the prophecy is accurate.

Wisdom

Was Gerald wise to bring such a word to R.T. with such strength and direction? And so publicly? He believed it to be God's word. And still does. Westminster Chapel was not completely changed in the way the prophetic word appears to imply. But on one night in Westminster, the prophetic picture was fulfilled. And at the Chapel, God moved. The meetings changed. R.T. changed considerably.

It may be Gerald got carried away with the strength of what he was saying. There were elements that were fulfilled. And elements that perhaps were not, or not in the way that was expected. Fodder for the bloggers. But on a night when two words appear to have been completely accurate, maybe Gerald can be forgiven for over-emphasising a third situation.

The proof of Gerald's prophetic influence is that the friendship with R.T. has remained solid. R.T. states that he has always liked Gerald. He appreciates his ministry and has joked that with Gerald's oratory and R.T.'s theology, they could have saved England!

It's a joke at Gerald's expense of course. R.T. is a strong Calvinist, believing in God's sovereign work. Gerald, influenced in particular by Roger Forster, is Arminian, with a firm belief that man has a good deal of free will in influencing the world around.

God's Words

Gerald has to always remember that any words he brings are God's words, not his. That way, he doesn't get hurt if the words are rejected. As with Peter Furler, the lead singer of the Newsboys in the States, who refuses to listen to Gerald at the time. He is struggling with his faith and doesn't want any word from God. He later accepts the words, though, and to this day they are posted on the back of the door of his bathroom.

Or the time when Gerald, in his role as advisor to the BBC on religious programming, finds himself sitting near television executive Michael Grade at a dinner. Again he feels a prompting from God to bring a prophetic word. But Grade is ahead of him. He knows Gerald's reputation and quickly rushes from the room announcing loudly, 'I don't believe in that stuff! I don't believe in anything! I don't believe in anything!'

Strange for the then director of the BBC to declare a complete lack of belief in anything whatsoever!

Gerald feels he heard God speak to him early in his ministry, specifically about the prophetic. On his own one day, Gerald hears God say to him, 'Son, all you have said so far, you have been willing to say. But I want to ask you, will you speak for me and say things you don't want to say?'

How could he respond in any other way than 'Yes'?

Immediately after that day, Gerald is tested on that very point, while he is a guest speaker at another church.

'There are two people here in an adulterous relationship,' says Gerald. 'If you come clean tonight, God will forgive you and give you a new start.'

Not the easiest thing to bring prophetically. And when no one responds, even harder.

A few days later, the pastor of the church resigns, having been in an adulterous relationship with his secretary. Both had been in the meeting.

New Zealand

Lake Taupo is beautiful. With a surface area of 616 square kilometres (238 miles) and 186 metres (610 feet) deep at its deepest point, it's impressive too. Gerald is lying on his hotel bed after a tiring day. He's been looking out at the scenery, and his mind is still on the size of the lake. Suddenly he's sobbing uncontrollably. God impresses on him a new picture. One of an earthquake. An immense, destructive force. But where? Here? On the lake?

Move on a day, and Gerald is spending a relaxing evening with Kiwi friends. The television is on; there's an advert. Not just any advert. One about what to do if there is an earthquake.

'Are these ads common?' asks Gerald.

'Not at all. Only if the authorities fear there may be an earthquake. The big one they fear is at Lake Taupo.'

'Where was I yesterday?' asks Gerald.

His travelling companion confirms it. Lake Taupo.

Gerald is sobbing again.

That same evening, Gerald shares his thoughts on what God has said. Not a prophecy as such. But clearly a word of warning about an earthquake.

The Christian community take it seriously and start to pray. If there is an earthquake under the lake it will flood the whole region. Prayer meetings are held up and down the lakeside. By the time Pioneer leader and children's minister Ishmael visits, the churches are united in regularly praying and fasting for God to stop the earthquake. Ishmael is strongly impacted by their faith and fervency.

The earthquake never happens. Good news for the 'heresy hunters'. Another story about Gerald. But is this an incorrect prophetic word? Or does God answer the prayers of thousands and avert an earthquake?

Gerald's good friend Peter Lyne is with him in New Zealand during this time. Peter has a different take on what happens. He's not sure Gerald is right to emphasise Lake Taupo, simply because that is where God gives him the picture. At that time, Gerald and Peter and the team are journeying from Lake Taupo to the South Island, and their next stop is Christchurch. Could it be Gerald is seeing a different earthquake – the one that devastates Christchurch in 2011?

14

TORONTO

Gerald remembers exactly where he is when he first hears about what is happening in Toronto. He's just preached at the Vineyard Church in south-west London and is at lunch with the leader of the Vineyard UK movement, John Mumford. As the conversation goes on, Gerald asks how John's wife Ellie is.

'Oh, I'm so sorry, I should have told you – she's out in Toronto.'

'Oh. Is that with relatives there?'

'No. Not at all. Haven't you heard?'

John begins to relate to Gerald all the recent happenings.

It is 20 January 1994 when Randy Clark first speaks at the Toronto Airport Christian Fellowship. Randy has been in a number of meetings with Rodney Howard-Browne, where one of the manifestations of ministry has been 'holy laughter'.

By the end of the meeting at Toronto, the majority of the congregation are on the floor. Some appear to be laughing uncontrollably, some are rolling around the floor. Others are shaking, unable to stop. There is an awareness of the presence of the Holy Spirit in a special way. The meeting goes on well past the time it is meant to finish. The pastor, John Arnott, asks Randy

Clark to stay on. That is the start of two months of daily meetings.

As people begin to hear of what is happening – not just the laughter and shaking, but deep repentance, heartfelt worship, and changed lives – they begin to come.

First of all from other parts of North America. Then from other countries, including an excited Ellie Mumford who is, in her own words, 'never slow to go to a party'!

As Gerald finishes lunch with John Mumford that day, he is convinced. As he sits there, he's aware of the familiar prompt of the Holy Spirit. This is of God. He's seen a degree of this before, but this sounds bigger; it sounds like God has a bigger plan for his church. He calls one of his leaders back at Cobham.

'It's going to happen to us. It's going to happen tonight. But I don't want you to mention Toronto. I don't want you to tell the story. Let's just see what God does.'

There's history here. The meetings at Cobham over the years have often been noisy affairs. People falling to the floor; shouting and shaking. So a lot of what Gerald is hearing from John Mumford is both new and not so new at the same time.

By the time Gerald has travelled back from London that day, the meeting has started. There, in front him, are people all over the floor. Some still. Others are rolling around. And there's the laughter. So much laughter. At the end of the meeting, some of the more 'prim and proper' members of the church are seen to be on the floor, unable to stop laughing, unable to get up, unable to go home.

Later that evening, as Gerald relaxes with a glass of Australian Cabernet Sauvignon, one of his favourite wines, he ponders again the day that has just transpired. These are moments that will be recorded in church history, he thinks. And for those that were on the floor tonight, changed lives. God has done some work in a moment that otherwise may have taken years. By His Holy

Spirit, God has worked miracles tonight, freeing up members of his congregation, setting them free from fears and doubts. There's a prayer of thanks on his lips as he climbs the stairs to bed.

Ellie Mumford

Ellie acts as something of a catalyst for this move of God when she gets home. In particular, as she shares what God has done with the leadership at Holy Trinity Brompton (HTB), a well-known Anglican church, the same phenomenon begins. One of the early 'receivers' of this blessing is Nicky Gumbel, the Alpha Course leader, and now vicar at HTB.

For Ellie, one of the keys to this particular blessing is the refreshing it brings to tired leaders. As Gerald relates, the church in the UK had lost its way as far as the general population is concerned. This move of God brings the church back into focus in many places – and it certainly picks up a lot of press coverage.

None more so than HTB. Gerald recalls a conversation with Sandy Millar, then vicar at HTB, when the HTB press officer, Mark Elsdon-Dew comes in. Mark is excited.

'The *Daily Express* are here. The *Daily Mail* are here. The *Telegraph* are here. The BBC are here!'

As quick as anything, Sandy Millar replies, 'I hope Jesus is here!'

And that's it, isn't it? Much of the criticism of the so-called Toronto Blessing relates to a possible over emphasis on the manifestations and the response to them, and not so much talk of Christ's salvation. Some of the manifestations such as barking or roaring like an animal appear extreme. Perhaps they are. And possibly unhelpful for others identifying this as something genuinely of the Holy Spirit.

Gerald is quick to defend this move of God, and when asked by Christian publishers, Word UK, to help present a video on the movement, he is pleased to help.

Rumours of Revival

Terry Virgo has arranged a conference at Brighton with some high-profile people attending, and that is Gerald's opportunity to sort out some of the interviews needed for the video. The interviews are wide-ranging and include a number of sceptics as well as those supporting what is happening. They include Bryn Jones supporting the move of the Spirit. This is one of the first reconciliations between Bryn and Gerald since the days of the Fabulous Fourteen.

Gerald and Terry Virgo share on video what has happened at various conferences as the manifestations first seen in Toronto begin to be seen in the UK. Ken Gott from Sunderland Christian Centre is on camera to tell of a particularly powerful move of the Holy Spirit in the Sunderland area.

There is talk of reconciled relationships. Testimonies of healed marriages. Stories of many returning to a faith in Christ. Support from the Pentecostal movement through an interview with Colin Dye of Kensington Temple. Support from R.T. Kendall, going on camera to record his view that this is of God, as well as his story of how he changed his mind.

And there's Rodney Howard-Browne on the video himself, pointing to Jesus and saying it's about God and not those who minister.

There's a section in the video that ties in the manifestations to scripture. And a potted history of earlier moves of the Holy Spirit in church history, with many of the same manifestations.

It is recorded that four thousand UK churches have been affected by the Toronto Blessing. And near the end of the video, there's an expectation from many of those interviewed that this is just the beginning. There are indeed rumours of revival and a hope from many that revival is just around the corner.

It doesn't arrive. Not in the way that people expect anyway. What does happen is a stirring among the churches, a reaching out over denominational boundaries and a preparation of God's people for evangelism. There is an increased boldness among the Christian community. And an increased acceptance, too, of the work of the Holy Spirit. It may not be revival in the UK but it is revival in the church. Not something that should be dismissed lightly. Boldness in the Holy Spirit has a way of outworking into society.

Gerald points out the direct links between Toronto and the sudden growth in the Alpha Course. He argues that there is indeed revival – just not a localised one such as we have seen in past decades in Wales and in the Hebrides.

And as Wendy Virgo puts it in the video: with all God is doing, the church is venturing on an 'unpredictable adventure'. That's the best kind.

The Pastor's Pastor

While this is happening in the UK, in the US all is not as it should be. Whereas, in the UK, the move of the Holy Spirit has brought considerable reconciliation among leaders, in the US, there is a separation. John Wimber feels unable to recognise the Toronto church as a continuing member of the Vineyard movement he leads, due to some of the manifestations.

This puts John Arnott, the pastor, in a bit of a spot. He turns to Gerald. Would Gerald be willing to take on the role of pastoring him? It is unexpected, and Gerald feels totally unprepared. Often these are the best ministries to have, though. You can't do it yourself, so you need to lean on God. Gerald does just that, and for a period of five years, he travels out to Toronto, not just to speak publicly, but to minster privately to the senior pastor of Toronto Airport Church.

South Korea

It's common for Gerald to stop preaching mid-flow and bring a prophetic word he feels God may be saying to someone.

One evening at Toronto, Gerald feels God speaking particularly to anyone in the meeting from South Korea. He's seen a few in the congregation. What he hasn't appreciated is that as many as three hundred are visiting from South Korea that night. They come to the front of the meeting, Gerald prophesies over them, and goes on with the meeting.

Well, he tries to. The noise of three hundred Korean Christians continuing to cry out to God throughout the meeting means that this particular preach from Gerald is lost to history!

Elim

One of the greater challenges Gerald and his fellow pioneers have had to face over the years is the challenge from the traditional Pentecostal churches, especially the Elim movement. In the early days, they didn't take kindly to the radical messages from Arthur Wallis, calling people out of their churches to establish something new. They felt that they already had the structure and the understanding of the work of the Holy Spirit for that to be unnecessary. Gerald was one of the louder voices in those early years to speak of coming out of denominations, and this brings him to the attention of Elim.

In the early 1990s there is a thawing of relationships, which has allowed Gerald and his fellow leader, Steve Clifford, to meet with three Elim leaders, including Wynne Lewis, head at that time of the Elim movement. The first meeting is in the restaurant on the twenty-eighth floor of the London Hilton. The meeting is frosty, to say the least. Gerald doesn't want to meet again, but is persuaded by his friend Steve to attend a second meeting.

The same restaurant. The same hotel. But something is different.

Gerald asks how they are. They burst out laughing.

'You've been to Toronto, haven't you? How was it?'

Wynne bursts out laughing again. His two colleagues are already giggling uncontrollably.

'I can't tell you much about Toronto', says Gordon, one of the other leaders, 'but I can tell you a lot about the carpet!'

The meeting is completely different. Wynne finds it hard to keep on topic. At one point, he stuffs a napkin into his mouth to try and stop the laughing. The work of the Holy Spirit has brought about reconciliation in a way that as leaders they have been unable to accomplish.

The Salvation Army

Toronto reaches many Christian groups within the UK. One of those groups is the Salvation Army.

It's the mid-nineties and there's a DAWN conference – Discipling A Whole Nation. Korean leader David Yonggi Cho, pastor of the biggest church in the world, is the main speaker. Gerald is on the stage. He looks out into the congregation and sees a number of men and women in uniform. Immediately, there's a battle going on within Gerald. The more he looks out at the Salvation Army captains, the more certain he is that he has a word for them.

But he doesn't want to deliver it. He's not sure he believes in all the Salvation Army are doing. And, more to the point, it's not his meeting to interrupt! But he does.

'I wonder whether our Salvation Army friends would mind standing? I believe God would say to you that He is bringing about something new from something old. He is calling you to go back to your roots. To rediscover the calling of the Salvation Army. As you do, God says, he will renew your movement.

'You will have wisdom as to when to wear the uniform and

when to take it off. Go back to your roots, and from those roots, all kinds of new things will grow!'

By now Gerald is in tears. As are many of the Salvation Army officers.

A few months later, Gerald is invited to speak at the first 'Roots' conference, organised by the Salvation Army.

Just before Gerald gets up to speak, the host whispers in Gerald's ear.

'Please can I ask you not to mention the Toronto Blessing?'

Gerald is cross. How can this man dictate what to say and what not to say? And with such short notice!

By now, the host is at the microphone and introducing Gerald. Then the most unusual thing happens. As the host prays, he begins to shake. There's no one else near him; no one is praying for him or laying hands on him. He can't carry on with his prayer, and then rather dramatically falls to the floor. With his hands raised in the air, he begins to roll around on the floor, laughing uncontrollably.

With no one else there to introduce him, Gerald takes the microphone anyway.

'He's just told me not to mention Toronto!' says Gerald.

There's laughter throughout the hall.

What follows is one of the most unusual Salvation Army meetings ever recorded. Not only the laughter and the shaking, but a deep Holy Spirit conviction. As the meeting moves on, there are many in tears. Some of the main leaders confess sexual sins. Others cry out to God for his Holy Spirit anointing.

The legacy is a revived Salvation Army. Numbers of new initiatives come out of the 'Roots' meetings, and the results are seen throughout the organisation. Churches are planted, the youth section reorganised, and the gospel is preached alongside the exemplary social action projects carried out by the Salvation Army.

Kingdom Now!

A powerful outworking of the Holy Spirit. People changed. Relationships restored. God surprising His people.

This is what is promised. This is what Gerald has been waiting for. So much of what is happening with the Toronto Blessing fits with Gerald's theology. A year earlier, Gerald had dusted off the chapters of *What on Earth is this Kingdom?* and re-issued the book as *Kingdom Now!* with some new material. Even this appears to have been a prophetic act, a prelude to a move of God. Gerald is able to say, 'This is that: this is God's Kingdom coming in; this is God breaking through into the here and now.'

Toronto doesn't herald revival. The video's question is ultimately answered. No, there may have been rumours of revival, but no long-term results in the nation. Many pastors are disappointed; some feel let down by God.

Many more remain grateful though. God has moved in his church. He has loosened things up. He has removed some of the religious straitjackets within the churches. He has brought in a laughter that is good for the church, repentance for many, and a closer walk with God for many more.

Perhaps most importantly, there is a working across boundaries, a breakdown of denominations. For this at least, the church in the UK can be thankful.

And as for Gerald, the strengthening of cross-denominational relationships brings some unexpected results.

15

THE LAMBETH CONNECTION

'Putting two coffins together does not produce a resurrection.'

So says Gerald in one of his early sermons. It's a comment at the time about the Presbyterian and Congregationalist merger, but is just as true, as far as he is concerned, in a wider context. Gerald is blistering in his attacks on the religious and irrelevant. And as he speaks, he is attacking the established church – none more so than the Church of England.

Much of Anglicanism in the 1960s was indeed irrelevant: religious services, devoid of life. The evangelical wing of the church was at a low point; the liberals appeared to have won.

Move on past Toronto and there's a very different picture. The evangelical and charismatic wing of the church is alive and well. The present Archbishop of Canterbury (at the time this book is being written) is a product of Holy Trinity Brompton.

But even before then, Gerald finds himself mixing with the Anglican hierarchy in ways a younger Gerald would have been surprised at. In fact, in ways a younger Gerald would probably have spoken against!

More than One, Less than a Handful

It's the early nineties. Gerald has had a long day at an evangelist's conference in Derbyshire. He's out at a restaurant late in the evening, winding down with his good friends Noel Richards and Ravi Zacharias.

It's a good meal, so late to bed.

At 5.30 a.m. Gerald wakes. He feels sharp, fully alive. There is no residue from the late night or the full conference day. He senses a particular anointing of the Holy Spirit on him.

Pen and paper in hand, he begins to write.

'This is for the Archbishop of Canterbury. He's bringing back more than one and less than a handful to evangelise the country.' That's it. Pen down. Head back on the pillow, before another busy day begins.

Gerald's not sure what to do with this word. He speaks to an Anglican leader at the conference about it, but it isn't clear the man understands. Gerald has no contact with the Archbishop of Canterbury and he doubts that he will be known by him. Well, if this is of God, He'll find a way . . .

A week later, there's a phone call. It's Michael Green, the Anglican theologian. Michael has been out in Canada for a while, working as Professor of Evangelism at Regent College, Vancouver. He is asking Gerald to meet up with a friend of Michael's who is moving to the area. At the end of the conversation, Gerald asks where Michael is.

'I'm visiting the UK at the moment.'

Suddenly it all fits.

'You're with the Archbishop of Canterbury, aren't you? It's a new evangelism initiative you're helping with. There's more than one of you but less than a handful.'

Stunned silence.

'How . . . How do you know? This is absolutely classified

information! If some people in the church hear of this, it will be dead before we start. I must ask you, Gerald. How on earth did you hear of this?'

Gerald explains that God woke him up at 5.30 one morning and gave him a prophetic word for the Archbishop.

Meeting George

George Carey has not long been Archbishop when he begins to plan for a Decade of Evangelism. Michael Green is asked to return from Canada to act as advisor.

When Michael shares Gerald's prophetic word with George Carey, George believes there is no doubt it is from God. It is the confirmation he is looking for.

'This has to be the Lord', says George. 'Gerald's given us such a hard time over the years. And now, unknowingly, he's endorsing this!'

More contact follows. Michael and Rosemary Green become regular attendees at Gerald and Anona's soirees at Clive House. It is at a New Year's Eve party that Michael begins to explain what George intends with the establishment of the Lambeth Partnership, a vehicle for the special projects of the Archbishop.

Gerald feels he should contribute towards this Decade of Evangelism and sends in a small amount he has received through royalties from a book. An invitation to the Lambeth Partnership event follows. As the Archbishop welcomes everyone, special mention is made of Gerald and Anona. In terms of financial gift, Gerald's amount must have been at the smaller end, but in terms of effect on the nation, the Archbishop is recognising a greater contribution.

The Archbishop begins to talk of new initiatives, including groups in the home.

'Of course you were doing this in the 1970s, weren't you Gerald?'

he says to all assembled, much to Gerald's embarrassment, and, if he's honest, his appreciation!

Gerald and Anona continue to attend events at Lambeth Palace. A most unlikely Christian alliance. And proof God has a sense of humour.

The Archbishop's Tears

Fair enough. George Carey is a strong evangelical. His successor, Rowan Williams, is from a different background. Gerald and Anona assume that their attendance at Lambeth Palace events will cease and that certainly, there will be no ongoing friendship with the new Archbishop. But it can't be further from the truth.

Gerald and Anona are welcomed by Rowan and Jane Williams as both friends and confidantes. What has begun with the previous Archbishop continues, but even more so.

It's late on a Friday in November 2012. Rowan Williams has just given a brilliant talk at a Lambeth Partnership event. Gerald is astounded that he has the ability to do so, bearing in mind that earlier in the day he has had to address the Anglican General Synod after they have turned down his proposals for women bishops.

As people are leaving, Rowan is at the door, giving his usual handshakes.

Gerald and Anona reach the door. Gerald reaches out his hand. Something more surprising happens than a handshake. Gerald is suddenly enveloped within the Archbishop's robes. As the Archbishop hugs him, Gerald whispers in his ear, 'That was a great talk Rowan, especially after the hell of a week you have just been through.'

What happens next is even more surprising. Rowan begins to cry, weeping on Gerald's shoulder. At a moment when the leader of the Church of England is at his most vulnerable, a supposed rebel and renegade from the house church movement is the one to bring comfort and encouragement.

With Justin Welby's appointment as Archbishop and with his background being Holy Trinity Brompton, Gerald and Anona continue to enjoy a good relationship with the Archbishop of Canterbury. At the 2014 Lambeth Partnership conference, the Archbishop asks Gerald for a copy of his latest book, as he wants to make use of it in a pastoral situation.

What the younger Gerald would make of all this is not recorded here. The fact that God has a sense of humour and remains God of each and every Christian tradition, is.

Every Tribe and Tongue

Christian sociologists argue that a lot of the work of the house church movement has been amongst predominantly white and middle-class society. Gerald is keenly aware that Christianity in the UK is much more than that. He has the privilege of being part of a Council of Reference for Matthew Ashimolowo, leader of possibly the largest church in the UK, the predominantly black Kingsway International Christian Centre.

The black worship leader Noel Robinson is a close friend of Gerald. A British-born man of Afro-Caribbean heritage, Noel has successfully crossed over many of the cultural expressions of worship, enabling him to lead worship at Christian events across the world. Much of this has been in recent years, and in particular, since Gerald prayed for him publicly.

Noel had been aware of Gerald and his prophetic ministry from the latter years of March for Jesus, when Noel was part of Graham Kendrick's worship band. From a black church in London, and acutely aware of the disconnect between the black and white churches in the UK, Noel has felt for many years that God was going to use him in some way to bridge the gap.

Move forward to a meeting at Kensington Temple with David Yonggi Cho as the main speaker. Gerald is on the stage.

Part way through the meeting, Gerald takes the microphone. Noel is part of the worship band that night and Gerald calls for Noel to join him. Having just prayed for someone else and poured a cup of water over him, Noel is slightly concerned when Gerald asks for a cup with oil in it!

Gerald is not someone who usually pours a whole cup of oil over someone, but, risking a claim for the dry cleaning bill, he does so. Christian singers and vocal coaches David and Carrie Grant are on the stage that night. David notices Noel's rather lovely black suede shoes and rushes to cover them before the oil gets that far! The whole cup of oil goes over Noel, staining his shirt and suit.

'Noel, I see God pouring blessing upon blessing on you. In abundance. Running over. You will receive an anointing that will take you to the nations! You will be a bridge to many different cultures. And you're going to see breakthrough in the United States. You will break through barriers. You will break through cultures!'

Noel records this moment as pivotal in all God has subsequently done in his ministry. Within three months, he is invited to the States. Contacts there lead him to being signed up to Integrity Music; he is one of the few black worship leaders to have such a contract.

Back home, Noel has regularly led worship at Spring Harvest as well as taking the lead for the National Day of Prayer at Wembley. 'Gerald's prophecy over my life wasn't new to my spirit,' says Noel, 'I had felt that cross-cultural call strongly. But that night at Kensington Temple was the strongest of confirmations. The word about visiting the States, and then the invitation to go there made the word stronger in me. Twenty years on, by God's grace, I'm leading across cultures and across countries.'

The Pope

Gerald and the Archbishop of Canterbury? Possibly. Gerald and the black church? Of course. Gerald and the Pope? You've got to be kidding!

But it's true. In 2005, through Gerald's connections with some in the UK Roman Catholic hierarchy, he is approached by them on behalf of Pope Benedict to ask Cliff Richard to perform at one of their massive youth gatherings in Cologne. Cliff duly obliges, as do the band Delirious?, singing to 1.3 million youth. And Gerald has a selfie to prove he was on the same stage as the Pope.

John Noble puts Gerald's connections with the great and the good down to his inbuilt confidence linked to his God-given prophetic gift. Gerald has often sought out certain leaders and politicians to bring a word of knowledge or a prophecy – usually encompassed with words such as, 'If God were to speak to you, I feel he'd be saying . . .' Others have sought out Gerald, especially when encouraged to do so by their fellow celebrities, based on the ministry Gerald has brought in the past.

But if people were to think that on occasion Gerald is running after someone important they would be proved wrong. John Noble points to a powerful gift of discernment, which warns Gerald to keep away from some. And so Gerald has kept clear of a number of scandals and rumours that would otherwise have tainted his own ministry.

Mention should be made of one of the more unusual church-based friendships. As recorded earlier, Gerald is strongly Arminian and R.T. Kendall strongly Calvinist. But a firm friendship has developed which continues to this day.

Gerald first hears R.T. speak at the Leadership '84 conference. Impressed with the talk, Gerald is quick to compliment R.T., and their friendship begins. Based on relationship, rather than theology, it has stayed strong despite the challenge from others regarding the Spring Harvest prophecy.

R.T. can't help but tease Gerald regarding his theology. 'The big mystery is how he got Anona. Wow, did he ever hit it hugely when he got her – enough to make him a Calvinist!'

The Parliamentary Connection

It's 1995 and Gerald has felt for a while that he has a particular prophetic word for John Major, then Prime Minister. But he's not about to write to Major and simply be seen as some sort of crank. He 'parks' the prophecy. If God has a hand in it and it's not Gerald's imagination, He'll sort out the 'how'.

There's a meal at a restaurant. A few friends are with Gerald, as is a senior politician in Prime Minister John Major's Cabinet. Gerald has forgotten the prophecy, but is reminded of it as the meal goes on and he gets talking to the politician. Gerald realises this is the opportunity he needs to get the word through to John Major, especially as the politician is a close friend of the Prime Minister.

Part way through the evening, Gerald leans over to the man and, conscious of his cautious Christian persuasion, says, 'How are you with prophecy?'

'Try me.'

'Well,' says Gerald, 'I feel God is prompting me to say to you that the Prime Minister is thinking of doing something that has never been done before, and he is unsure whether to do it. He needs to know he should do it – God will be with him, and it will work out.'

Suddenly this cautious, Conservative (with a big and small 'c') politician grabs hold of Gerald and gives him a hug. Banging his hand onto Gerald's knee, he says, 'You have no idea what this means! No idea!'

Soon afterwards, he leaves the restaurant.

'Gerald, what on earth was that about?' ask his fellow diners.

'Well,' says Gerald, 'I don't exactly know. Let's see.'

A short while afterwards, whilst remaining as Prime Minister, John Major resigns as leader of the Conservative party. This is the first and only time there has been a leader of the country who has not also been the leader of his political party. John Major has been regularly under pressure from the Euro-sceptics within his party, so he lays down the challenge. Neither Michael Heseltine nor Michael Portillo, both expected to challenge, do so. Only John Redwood, then Secretary of State for Wales, challenges Major. And Redwood is roundly beaten. John Major is victorious; he returns to the leadership of his party with the worst of the infighting over.

Gerald's attended a few functions at Downing Street since then, most recently as a representative of Christian influencers and pioneers.

It's not just the British government that Gerald has influenced. He's in Paris one time, working with the church planter Charlie Cleverly. Gerald sees a lady a few rows back, clearly being touched through the Holy Spirit. Gerald goes over and prays for her, at which point she falls to the floor. It's only afterwards that Gerald is told she's the Minister of Finance in the French government.

16

THE ROYAL CONNECTION

Gerald's parties over the years have regularly included the celebrated and the famous. This has often meant that Cliff Richard is on the guest list, alongside the late Alvin Stardust, politicians such as Lord Mawhinney, and well- known Christian leaders such as R.T. Kendall and David Pawson. These two famously made up their differences at one of Gerald's parties. R.T. comments that 'it's hard to maintain enmity with someone when you are talking to them with a plate of food in one hand and a glass of wine in the other!'

One of the most remarkable connections remains Gerald's link with the royal family of Romania.

The Prophecy

Gerald's long-term friend David Taylor was a conveyancer. In the early 1970s, sitting next to Gerald in a meeting, a well-known preacher with a prophetic ministry lays his hands on David and speaks:

'You will have a ministry to the Royal Family.'

Gerald is concerned. This is a middle manager in a solicitors' practice. Surely such a word, if it is correct, should be for Gerald himself? After all, Gerald is the full-time pastor. David has just come along to the meeting as a friend.

Perplexed, the young and somewhat arrogant Gerald dismisses the prophecy as a bit of a wild word and no more is said.

Move forward twenty years. Gerald gets a phone call. It's David.

'Gerald, I've just been told about a job. Princess Margareta, Prince Charles' cousin and the Crown Princess of Romania, is looking for a UK representative for her charity. Do you I think I should apply?'

'This is the prophecy, David! This is it! Of course you should go for it!'

David gets the job.

Over the next few years, Gerald gets to know Princess Margareta by way of various charity functions. Then there's a Youth With A Mission conference in Geneva and Gerald is the guest speaker. David decides to come along as well.

'David, why are you coming to this? You hate conferences!'

'I want you to meet Princess Margareta's parents, King Michael and Queen Anne. King Michael is cousin to our Queen. They live in Geneva. I want you to pray for them.'

'I know they live there. But David, you know full well that's not how it works! You don't even touch a Royal unless it's a handshake. You certainly never lobby a member of the Royal Family – and asking to pray for them would be lobbying!'

David smiles. 'Let's see.'

Travelling Man

The flight is on time. As Gerald stares out of the window on that short trip to Geneva, he has time to reflect. How did he ever get to be speaking to royalty in the way he now is? And politicians? And even the Archbishop of Canterbury? He smiles. God is fulfilling

His word, making of Gerald something that in his wildest dreams Gerald could never have imagined.

By this time he's been travelling around the world on a regular basis for a number of years. From a first trip to the States with some of the Fabulous Fourteen, to teaching and preaching in many countries. Gerald is grateful.

He's travelled to many places, spoken in many countries. He's been to several parts of Africa, to South America, and through most of Europe. He's spoken at or led major conferences in France, Italy, Spain, Norway, Sweden, Malta, the United States, Canada, Mexico, Australia and New Zealand.

Not that these travels have been without sacrifice. Many a time, he has had to leave Anona behind as the boys were growing up. Gerald remembers one set of meetings where he clearly was feeling some conflict with having left his family on their own over a weekend, and this comes out in his preaching that night. At the end of the meeting, an old man moves towards him. There's a determined look in his eye. Waving his walking stick in Gerald's direction, he says, 'Young man, I have a word for you! You know, young man, God is a perfect Father, and He has many wayward children. Do you think you are going to do better?'

It lifts a load from Gerald's mind at a crucial moment when travel is picking up. His boys will be cared for by a Father who has a greater love than Gerald can ever have.

As the years go by, Gerald begins to get better at managing the travel and his family. His boys have done well. Anona has appreciated Gerald's ministry. And the miles apart have always brought about a greater appreciation of their marriage and family whenever Gerald has returned.

Geneva

The plane lands. Two hours later, David and Gerald are in the

Geneva home of the Romanian Royal Family. The room they are in overlooks the lake. The majestic mountains in the background and the manicured lawns outside the window create a beautiful picture.

It's a mid-morning meeting. They wait. And wait.

Forty-five minutes later, a flustered Queen Anne comes into the room.

'I'm so sorry to keep you. So sorry.'

She is closely followed by King Michael. It turns out that they have had some troubling family news that morning and have been trying to deal with it.

'It's not a problem, ma'am, we can go.' Gerald and David get up to leave.

'No. No! Stay! Please, sit down.'

An hour's meeting turns into two. Then three. They stay for a light meal. David is struggling to believe what is happening. This is the Royal Family of Romania. They never change schedules. They never ask people to stay. But here is Gerald being asked to stop for the whole afternoon.

The talk is general, but as Gerald and David make to leave, Queen Anne asks Gerald to pray for them. He does so. A pretty general prayer, but with a few extra words under his breath. 'Lord, please change their lives!'

As Gerald gets up from the beautifully embroidered armchair, he gives the couple a book by the theologian Ravi Zacharias. Both the king and queen are strongly academic so Gerald reckons they may well read it. As an afterthought, Gerald also leaves them a copy of his autobiography *An Intelligent Fire*, because David is mentioned in it.

The Meeting

Three weeks later, Gerald gets a call from David.

'Queen Anne wants a meeting with you. She's getting permission from Queen Elizabeth to enter the country and will come to your house.'

'But why, David? What for?'

'I'm not sure. She hasn't told me.'

A week later, David, his wife Carrie and Anona are in the house praying. Gerald is in the garden, sitting under the oak tree with Queen Anne. She speaks for a while of family matters, as well as her concern for the British Royal Family. But Gerald knows there must be more.

'Excuse me asking, ma'am, but why is it you have come? How can I help?'

'It's your book. I've read it twice in the last three weeks. I didn't realise. I never knew. I always thought Christianity was to do with rules and dogma. And I hate rules and dogma! But it's not like that . . . He cares. He cares for me. His friendship is for simple people like me!'

That day, in Gerald's garden, he prays with the Queen of Romania to find a new faith. A friendship and faith for simple people. Like Queen Anne.

Another week on, Princess Margareta calls Gerald.

'Gerald, what have you done to my mother?'

'What do you mean, ma'am?'

'She's different. She's speaking of her faith. She seems to have found her vocation.'

The Tour

While Gerald is on a speaking tour, out of the blue Queen Anne contacts him again and asks if she can join him. What do you say to a Queen when she asks to speak on your preaching tour? 'Yes' is the only possible answer, of course.

The meeting hall in Bristol is packed. Gerald hasn't told the congregation about his special guest, but part way through his preach, he stops to introduce her.

'I have a very special guest tonight. She's going to talk for a few minutes. Please welcome Queen Anne of Romania.'

The congregation hesitate. Then applaud. Did he really just say Queen Anne? There's a queen speaking?

For a few minutes, she tells her story: of driving ambulances in the Second World War; of supporting the exiled French Army; of being thrown out of Romania by the Communists: of how the country has been devastated as a result; and of how healing is coming. And then she says: 'I just want to say to you God is real. I have found God to be real in my life and there's nothing I want more than to live minute by minute for Jesus Christ.'

A quiet murmur goes through the building. People begin to clap. The applause gets louder. People are standing on their feet cheering. A Queen and her faith. A simple friendship for, as the Queen herself puts it, a simple person. A life changed, and a vocation found.

'Isn't He Wonderful?'

A strange thing happens at that Bristol meeting. Near the end of her talk, it looks like the Queen is going to faint. She is visibly swaying. Cognisant of the need to help her, and aware at the same time that you don't touch Royalty, Gerald shuffles forward and gently puts his hand on her back.

The next night, they're at a meeting in Surrey. The same thing happens. The Queen looks to be fainting, so Gerald puts his hand on her back to keep her upright.

Later that evening, during the meal, Gerald asks the Queen what happened.

'Well, last night, I put it down to nerves. I haven't spoken publicly in a while, so I assumed my nerves were getting the better of me and I was going to faint. But tonight I was fine. There were no nerves. However, the same thing happened. What do you think it could have been? I never get fainting fits or anything like that.'

Gerald begins to explain about the Holy Spirit and some of the things that are happening at that time in the Toronto renewal.

'So you think this is the Holy Spirit?'

'Yes ma'am, I do.'

'Well,' says the Queen, 'Isn't He wonderful?'

Fairmile Court

One more meeting. It's a Pioneer leaders' conference at Fairmile Court. Gerald's asked the Queen to arrive a little before lunchtime, and to share her story with his leaders.

But this is 'Toronto' time. By the time the Queen arrives, there are bodies all over the floor! Some people are rolling around, others are laughing; some are in tears, and many are 'drunk' in the Spirit. God is at work.

Gerald glances out of the window. There's a chauffeur-driven car coming up the drive. The Queen! Gerald has forgotten she's coming. What to do? There are a number of people laid out on the carpet next to the meeting room door. No way out that way. Gerald goes through the window, around the back of the house, and back in through the kitchen, just in time to reach the front door of the conference centre as the Queen arrives. They have a cup of tea in the library. And there is a slightly better-ordered group of leaders after lunch as the Queen speaks.

But you get the feeling she really wouldn't have minded.

17

THE CITY AND THE CHURCH

Gerald's passion is the church and the kingdom – the Bride of Christ and her place in God's purposes. A triumphant, pioneering church, demonstrating the supernatural, life-changing King of Kings. A church that leads, that speaks out, that reaches out. A church that heals. Being all Christ intended the church to be.

For the church to be all she should be, she needs to be effective in major cities and small villages, in church meetings and on Monday mornings in the workplace. And if the church is to be all she should be, the church needs to be effective in the corridors of power. It is a natural move, therefore, for Gerald to begin to plan meetings in central Westminster at the time of the Toronto Blessing.

If the Church is being blessed through the Holy Spirit, then there is a need, says Gerald, to take that blessing out to the world around. If the Church is to reach that world, how can Parliament be excluded? Why are there so few major churches in the centre of London?

What can be done?

Marsham Street

It's 1996, two years since the birth of the Toronto Blessing. Gerald is praying. Aware of the earlier prophecies about reaching London, he's sure it's the right time to take a step of faith, possibly meeting in London for a few months. Maybe up to four times a week. His local church has been generous with the money that's needed. But where to meet?

He hears about Marsham Street, a circular church building near the centre of Westminster. It's owned by a Chinese church and available for hire.

Gerald and some friends are walking around, talking about the practicalities. That's when Chin arrives. Chin is the caretaker. He asks Gerald what he's doing there. Gerald explains, and goes on to introduce himself.

'My name's Gerald. Gerald Coates.'

Chin looks on, his eyes getting wider and wider. He's slowly stepping back, away from Gerald. Suddenly he lets out a scream, loud and piercing, and falls to the floor.

It's fair to say it's not the usual response to meeting Gerald. In fact Gerald isn't sure what to do. It's not often he gets embarrassed, but he is now. Gerald pretends to continue looking at the building while the caretaker recovers and is helped by friends.

A few minutes later, Chin has recovered and Gerald asks him what happened.

'It was amazing. As you spoke and introduced yourself, I saw an angel, an enormous angel, right behind you, guarding your back. That's why I screamed. I've never seen anything like that. I'm just a caretaker. I don't see stuff like that!'

And with that, Chin screams again and, for the second time, hits the floor. Another angel! God's sense of humour.

Angels Again

Marsham Street is hired for four nights a week. The meetings are a success. No big names but a continual flow of new people come through the doors seeking a Holy Spirit anointing. Anything from 150 people to 500 people each night, four nights a week for a few months.

In fact the meetings attract not just people, but the press. Continuous meetings in the City of Westminster are unusual and the papers turn up to find out more. There's worship, teaching, stories and healing. There's a lot of answered prayer, with testimony each night of what God has done. It's a simple agenda, and one that God blesses.

It is during this time that a leader asks Gerald to pray for him. Gerald takes him up to the pastor's study in order to find some privacy.

When Gerald has finished praying for him, the man is speechless.

'What's the matter?' asks Gerald.

'Didn't you see? Didn't you see the angel?'

'Well, no,' says Gerald, 'I didn't. But I did hear someone come into the room. I assumed it was the Chinese pastor.'

'No one came into the room. There was an angel here. Right here. Right behind you as you were praying.'

As Gerald prays and thinks about these two angelic appearances, he feels that at least one of the reasons for their appearance is simply assurance. Things are a bit tough with his home church right now and he feels God is saying that He has Gerald's back. Some people have wanted to stab him in the back, but God assures Gerald that he isn't to worry about it. God is on the case and Gerald's back is protected. Gerald feels assured that God will sort out the attackers in His own way, and without any need for Gerald's intervention.

And God does sort it out. This book can't record the detail, due to the sensitive issues and individuals involved, but God well and truly protects Gerald's back. And his front for that matter!

Parliament Again

Gerald is getting bolder. Spurred on by the accuracy of his prophetic words for the Prime Minister John Major, Gerald is regularly catching up with Gary Streeter, MP. Gary is a charismatic Christian and welcomes the help and support Gerald and others can give him. Over the years, they have met regularly and Gary would sometimes call in for prayer at Gerald's home on his way down to his constituency in Devon.

On one of his visits to the House of Commons in 2009 to meet with Gary, Gerald sees the MP John Bercow. Suddenly there's a word. A clear word for him.

'Excuse me, Mr Bercow. You don't know me. I heard you at a Christian Solidarity Worldwide conference. I thought you were excellent.'

'Thank you.'

'Mr Bercow. I just feel to say that if Jesus Christ were able to stand here and talk to you, he'd be saying that promotion is about to come your way.'

'Oh. Er, thank you.'

And that is it. John Bercow has gone. Although not a Christian, Bercow is of Jewish descent and during that time, Gerald continues to hope that he will heed the prophetic word.

A month or two later, Bercow announces his decision to stand for Speaker of the House of Commons. He is successful.

Waverley Abbey House

It's surprising that someone as active as Gerald has time to consider other roles. But Gerald gets involved in a number of different

Christian initiatives and finds time to attend and chair various committees. Gerald has been supportive in helping a revamp of Fusion, the student mission organisation, and in encouraging Pete Greig with the 24/7 prayer initiative. More recently, in 2013, Gerald has been helping arrange flash mobs and prayer meetings in Parliament Square to highlight Christian persecution in Iraq and Syria.

Gerald has been known to tell people he's on CRAC. That's the Central Religious Advisory Council to you and me. He is there at a time when the BBC appears not to be fully aware of the number of churches there are in the UK. For the record, there are around 50,700 churches, compared to about 1,600 mosques. Together with the fact that the fastest growing churches are the charismatic ones, this is something Gerald is keen to ensure the BBC knows about and responds appropriately to.

One of Gerald and Anona's more radical decisions relates to Waverley Abbey House. Gerald has stepped down from the day-to-day running of Cobham Christian Fellowship, by now called Pioneer People. He is actively involved in London initiatives and, with Norman and Sheila having moved on, Gerald and Anona needed to move on from Clive House. Lakeside Drive, Esher, has become their new home.

Gerald has known Selwyn Hughes of Crusade for World Revival (CWR) for some years. Nevertheless, the invitation in 1998 from Chief Executive Officer John Muys is a real surprise. John wants Gerald and Anona to move to the CWR headquarters and help Waverley Abbey House find a new and clearer direction. Even Gerald with his prophetic leanings hasn't seen that one coming.

Gerald and Anona pray. Despite the fact that this has come as a surprise for them, they feel it is of God. Consequently, they sell Lakeside Drive and buy a flat in Westminster with some of the proceeds. This gives them somewhere to stay when they are involved with their various London initiatives, including Christians in Parliament, Marsham Street and working with the Lambeth Partnership.

Despite God's assurances, moving to Waverley Abbey House is a shock. They take over part of the upper floor as their accommodation, and Anona gets to work as Front of House Manager. Gerald's influence is seen with regard to direction and networking. With the help of his business friend Paul Williams, a new trust is set up for the house, with the publishing arm being run by others at CWR.

The whole tone of the place changes. From the formality of a conference centre, it moves instead towards a Christian house that facilitates conferences. Anona is quick to put coffee facilities into each of the bedrooms. The décor is improved and, as a consequence, it becomes a place where people want to stay.

The Pioneer and March for Jesus offices are moved there too, along with Gerald's long-suffering Personal Assistant. Once Gerald is sure of something, he becomes highly focused on it. His networking brings the house and its potential for conferencing to the notice of many new customers. One of the spin-offs from this time is Gerald's own Leaders' Round Table for apostles, prophets and leaders of larger new churches and church groupings. The meetings continue to this day, and are still held at Waverley Abbey House.

The early days at the House also include some staff issues – a policy of non-cooperation may best describe it. But over time, this too changes and the place becomes somewhere people want to work.

All this is to change again.

The New Appointment

By 2002, a new CEO has been appointed. It is a mistake. And it's a pretty disastrous one.

Following his appointment, Gerald and Anona befriend him, take him for meals and introduce him to the area, as he has moved from another part of the country. A good friendship seems to be developing. Until the night at the pub.

It's been a good evening. Gerald has been in best storytelling mode and there has been plenty of laughter along the way.

The three of them walk back to the house.

'Goodnight. See you in the morning.'

'Yes. About that. About tomorrow. It's time for you to go.'

Gerald and Anona don't understand.

'What do you mean?'

'It's time for you to leave. We can't have two ministries here. Gerald, people are seeing your ministry, as more important than Selwyn's. We can't have that. You have to go.'

'But Waverley Abbey House is first and foremost CWR! It's not us. We work with you, not against you!'

There is no movement from the CEO. Gerald and Anona are on their way.

Unfortunately, the new man very quickly upsets many of the staff. Resignations are regularly and openly being discussed.

It is at Sainsbury's where all this changes. Anona is shopping when the Chair of the Trustees sees her. Out it all comes. The decision. The staff potentially leaving. Gerald and Anona leaving. The turmoil within the office.

By the end of the next day, the CEO has left. Too late, though, for Gerald and Anona, who have by now made their own plans to move on.

18

PIONEER PEOPLE

In football parlance, he 'took his eye off the ball'.

All the excitement of Waverley Abbey House and the London initiatives, plus international travel, means that Gerald is not watching what is happening back home at Cobham.

If the March for Jesus and some of the London initiatives represent Gerald at his best, this chapter has to record Gerald at his lowest. What happens to Pioneer People at Cobham remains one of the most painful moments in Gerald's life. For Anona, the death of Pioneer People, for that's what it is effectively, is akin to a child dying.

A New Name, a New Day

It starts so well.

There is no doubt that at the time Cobham Christian Fellowship morphs into Pioneer People, things are powering ahead. It is a new church name for a new day. The church is growing, Gerald is heading up Pioneer Network, one of the best-known and fastest growing streams within the new church movement, and there is significant influence from both Gerald and from the church to the region and the nation. Pioneer People in Cobham is the flagship church of the movement: a dynamic new-style church with powerfully led worship from Noel Richards, great preaching and a strong application to daily life.

Mike Blount originally takes on the local leadership from Gerald. After a good start, he begins to struggle. Burnout. And he steps down from leadership.

With his increasingly international ministry, Gerald isn't there. Gerald is, of course, responding to Peter Lyne's prompting to lay down the local in order to take on more of a national role. That is the right thing to do. But Gerald, the encourager, the mentor, misses Mike's struggles until it is too late.

Tensions

As the 80s move into the 90s, first Martin Scott and then Stuart Lindsell take on the local leadership. They are good leaders. The church looks healthy. Up to six hundred people meeting on a good week.

Times change and the leaders change. The new leadership team feel that they need to expand in numbers. Eventually seven people are appointed, with four of that number more involved in the day-to-day running of the church. The seven – a mix of men and women, fluctuate in and out of leadership. Not necessarily married couples – a combination of marrieds, singles and one-half of marrieds in leadership together.

There it is. The new leadership team. A genuine mix of giftings and backgrounds, marrieds and singles together in leadership. It sounds utopian. But it isn't.

Tensions surface early on. It is a big leadership team. Perhaps too big. They reach out for assistance to three good friends of Pioneer – Roger Ellis, John Noble and Jeff Lucas.

Gerald is aware of the situation but feels his past leadership compromises his getting involved. Best to leave it to Roger, John and Jeff to sort out. The problem is, though, that after some while, the conclusion Roger, John and Jeff come to is that their advice is not going to be accepted.

By now, numbers on Sunday reflect the tensions. The high watermark of six hundred on a Sunday is long gone. Now it is around two hundred. Two hundred and fifty on a good day. Many leave. Many become occasional attenders. Despite moving to an excellent local theatre to meet, the numbers do not increase. That's when James Thwaites arrives.

Church Deconstruction

Deconstructionism. That's its technical title.

James Thwaites arrives from Australia in 2001. There is some confusion as to what church he belongs to. Some seem to think he is with Hillsong, a well-known and lively church stream based in Sydney, Australia. That's not the case. James was at Hillsong but has left some time ago. It seems Gerald doesn't check this out. Peter Lyne does. On the basis that Thwaites has no recommendation from a like-minded church, Peter doesn't let him in to speak at his churches, however Gerald does.

James Thwaites's message at this time could be considered both good and not so good. Good in recognising the problems within church and church meetings. Not so good with the remedy.

Thwaites deconstruction message identifies that pastors are getting onto a rollercoaster ride of church performance, that they are expected to entertain rather than preach a life-changing word from the Bible. Added to this, the church generally is failing to make inroads into the post-modern world we live in. Pastors are burning out and stepping down. The emphasis on a Sunday congregation is detrimental to the church in the world, the church in the pub, the church in the workplace.

All this may be true of many local churches at the start of the new millennium. But the solution proposed– a deconstruction of church – means closing the Sunday congregation. A renegotiation of the church contract is what is proposed. And that means, in actuality, tearing up the whole thing and starting again.

But to stop meeting as 'church', as a living body, to worship and hear God's word, is contradictory to the call in Scripture to meet together, to bring a song, a contribution from the Bible and so much more.

Right problem diagnosis. Wrong solution.

But to many congregations throughout the UK, this message is so welcome. For every struggling pastor and every small church failing to reach its neighbourhood, it offers an opportunity to get off the 'treadmill' of Sunday church. So they do.

But then they disappear.

The moment you stop meeting and introduce something less structured, with little or no leadership, you're in trouble. You no longer meet regularly. You no longer have an accepted format. Maybe you no longer have a leader. So, despite the best intentions, you die.

Many are the casualties of church deconstruction. Among them are the former members of Pioneer People.

Telling Signs

It seemed like the answer to their problems. Martin Scott, then leader of Pioneer People, is on the back cover of James Thwaites's first book, *The Church Beyond the Congregation*, recommending it. The second book, *Renegotiating the Church Contract*, is even more radical. And Gerald adds his endorsement to the cover. This proves to be a mistake.

James Thwaites is invited to speak at a number of the Pioneer churches, and then at the main leaders' conference.

If the internal leadership tensions at Pioneer People are the catalyst for decline, an acceptance of deconstruction teaching helps to finish off what once was one of the most flourishing and successful churches in the new church movement.

It's not right to blame Thwaites for the closure of Pioneer People, of course. Things have not been right for a while. The large leadership team is not working well together. There is pressure for change and there are disagreements within the team. Some are for adopting deconstruction teaching in its entirety; others are not so sure. But they do not take the advice from Roger Ellis, John Noble or Jeff Lucas. One of the key leaders feels he has to step down. He cannot agree to this apparent self-destruction of a dynamic church. He cannot watch it happen.

Things go from bad to worse. By the time the team feel they are no longer a team that can lead church as it has been, it is all but over. They decide to follow the deconstruction model, abandon Sunday church and seek to be church in the community. Gerald feels he is unable to change the direction. He has not been asked to. With even his best friend John Noble unable to help the leadership, Gerald can do little more than accept the inevitable.

The Golf Club

A meeting is arranged at the local golf club. Gerald and Anona – who have recently returned from Waverley Abbey House to the local area, and are now living in Bookham – are invited to attend, but not to lead.

Without clear leadership and clear direction, the meeting is anarchic. People stand up to say that 'church' is not a meeting on a Sunday, that they don't need church leaders, and that people should be left to choose what they want to do. There is anger, finger pointing, accusation; little effort is made to keep the church together.

As Gerald and Anona drive back that night with a good friend, it becomes too much for Anona. She breaks down in tears. Not just crying, but deep, deep sobs. Bending over in the car, Anona is unable to control the sobbing; it is more of a wailing. She is aching inside, crying out in grief as to what has happened. A deep grieving as if she has lost a child. And that's what it feels like to her. The loss of a child.

This is the night Pioneer People dies.

A Time of Jubilee

After the Golf Club meeting, it's all about trying to finish well.

The leaders call the church together for three nights of 'jubilee', reflective of the jubilee of the Old Testament when Israel release slaves and debt and return to their own homes.

Night one is a time to 'reflect'. Night two is a time to 'repent'. Night three is a time to 'release'.

Reflecting is therapeutic. There is much to give thanks for. Repentance is good, too, though in the context of that second night, Gerald feels it is too limited and too general to be effective. The third night is hard. Some of the more strident leaders are clear that this is a great step forward. But many of the congregation are confused. Why close a church just because it has run into problems? Meeting in homes and pubs? Sure. Community initiatives? Yes. But where is the direction? Where is the leadership?

Call it a time of jubilee if you like. It is the closure of a church.

Gerald recalls it as one of the most painful seasons of his and Anona's lives. Sometimes those in a congregation think that leaders are above hurt and emotion. It's not true of course. There's been prayer. God has done His healing work. But ask Gerald and Anona about Pioneer People and even today there's still a tear in the eye.

19

SEX

Sex is not an obsession with Gerald, but he does talk about it a lot! Of course, in the early days of the house church movement, because of his outspoken comments and radical views, Gerald was considered to be the one most likely to lose his way. On the contrary, he and Anona are still happily married, parents, and now grandparents as well. Others from that early new church movement have fallen, either morally or from faith, but Gerald is still going strong.

Not For Discussion

Back in the early days of the house church movement, talking about sex openly was not common, and was not really encouraged. Gerald's insistence on talking through issues such as a Christian response to masturbation often got him into trouble.

Picture the scene. It's early evening at a conference centre. The Fabulous Fourteen, those early leaders of the house church movement, have been in deep discussion for much of the day on the role of the apostle and prophet. As they sit down to dinner in the evening, Gerald leans back from the table and says:

'So Arthur. What's your view on masturbation? Is it okay for a Christian man to masturbate? Or should we discourage it?'

What, at that moment, the saintly Arthur Wallis thinks of this question is not recorded. But in all likelihood, being of an earlier generation and despite his pioneering, Arthur will not have been impressed by the turn in the conversation.

It seems that such conversations, accompanied with what are seen as risqué jokes, are part of the reason for 'the letter' from Arthur and Bryn Jones to the southern brothers in those early days, removing themselves from regular Christian fellowship with them. It doesn't stop Gerald talking about it though.

The 'M' Word

Gerald doesn't shy away from the battles. Others may not be willing to talk about masturbation, but it doesn't hinder Gerald.

His most recognised book *What on Earth Is this Kingdom?* was widely used by the early house church. Here too, there is discussion on masturbation. Is Gerald being controversial for the sake of it? He's often accused of such. But for him, the concern outweighs the controversy. These things need talking about. Scripture may be silent on masturbation, but the practice is common – and common among Christians, especially men. So who is going to speak on it? Gerald of course.

There is background here as well. Gerald's first book, written with Hugh Thompson, *Not Under Law*, is a strong presentation of God's grace. The theme follows through in most of Gerald's later books and, along with it, a genuine concern that generations of young Christian men are getting hung up on something that is not necessarily a sin. Gerald argues that masturbation for 'self-control' is very different to masturbation for 'self-gratification'.

So there you go. Ever the controversialist.

The Gay Debate

Gerald likes to say it as it is. He is on record debating against homosexuality by pointing out that male to male sex is unnatural. There is no appropriate orifice for a male penis apart from a female vagina. In a male to male relationship, the alternative orifice is not designed to be used in that way.

Gerald regularly challenges the notion that if you are two men or two women 'in love' with each other, it must be alright: 'We don't say it's okay for a grown man to say he has "fallen in love" with a 6-year-old-girl. If he had "fallen in love" with a 14-year-old-girl, we wouldn't accept it. If a man says he has "fallen in love" with his sister, we wouldn't agree to it. So why is it okay to say it's alright for a man to have "fallen in love" with another man?'

Gerald's book *Sexual Healing* carries on the debate. Gerald is more measured in print. The book gives a full and scripturally based argument for the problems of homosexuality.

Gerald points out that there is no scientifically proven reason for homosexuality. The 'gay gene' theory doesn't stack up. It is something 'men do', rather than what 'men are'. Gerald argues that young people, particularly young boys, often go through a stage of same-sex attraction and inquisitiveness, but most grow out of it. This stage is in danger of being exploited by the gay rights lobby.

With the government decision to push through same-sex marriage, marriage becomes whatever anyone wants it to be. It has lost its biblical moorings. With care and solid arguments, Gerald takes us through the minefields that exist in the gay rights debate. He lands solidly on the Bible as having the final say. His book will not make Gerald many friends from the gay rights brigade, but it is a welcome explanation full of biblical common sense in an increasingly lost and morally vacant world.

And if for a moment you think this is some sort of right wing fundamentalism without Christian compassion, remember that Gerald, supporting Dr Patrick Dixon, helped create one of the biggest and most successful AIDS charities in the UK.

Another Nathan

It's 2012 and Gerald is sending out a couple of messages on Facebook. As he finishes, he notices a group photo on the page of one of the young men in Pioneer. One of the faces in the photo stands out. Gerald hasn't met him before, but he senses God is about to do something in that particular man's life.

Through the wonders of Facebook, Gerald sends the young man a message. He feels to tell him, 'You are planning your exit but you need to know that God has other plans for you.'

That is it. Gerald doesn't expect to hear any more. He quite often sends prophetic words to people and doesn't require a reply – after all it's between them and God and up to them whether they want to respond to Gerald or not.

But this young man does respond. He says his name is Nathan and he needs to talk. Gerald invites him down to visit him and Anona at their house in Bookham. The visit is arranged, and Nathan arrives for the weekend.

It's a pretty ordinary time. Gerald finds Nathan to be very polite. He even helps with the dishes! But there's something going on under the surface. Ah well. If God is at work, reasons Gerald, it will come out somehow.

But it doesn't. The whole thing is rather uneventful. Nathan enjoys the weekend, visits the church and goes back home.

Gerald does invite Nathan to the Pioneer conference though, so a few weeks later, there's Nathan again. They get on well and Gerald ends up asking Nathan to consider moving down to the Bookham/Leatherhead area and becoming Gerald's new PA. Nathan accepts.

'But there's just one thing,' says Gerald. 'If you're working for me, I need to be sure there is nothing in your past that can embarrass me. Nothing that would possibly be found out and affect my own ministry.'

Suddenly, there's a look of horror on Nathan's face. He's nervous. Not sure where to look.

'Gerald. There is something.'

This is what Gerald has been waiting for. From the first meeting, Gerald has known there is something there that needs to be discussed. God brings these things out in his own time. What Gerald doesn't expect though, is the issue that Nathan is grappling with.

'Gerald, I'm a porn addict. I look at porn every day. Sometimes three or four times a day. I can't seem to break the habit. It's addictive. It started with just page three-type stuff, but now it's much more. When you sent me that Facebook message, do you remember what you said?'

Gerald thinks. 'Something about you were planning to exit something?' says Gerald.

'You actually said, "You are planning your exit but God has other plans for you." Your Facebook note arrived not long after I had constructed my suicide note to my parents. If I couldn't live for God because of my porn problem, I didn't want to live at all.'

There's silence. Then tears.

Gerald sits down next to Nathan and they begin to pray. Gerald's prayers are compassionate, yet firm. In Jesus' name, he breaks the power of the addiction. Nathan's willingness to be open about something so sensitive helps in breaking the power that pornography has over him. As Gerald prays, Nathan is delivered from the desire to look at porn on the internet.

And so begins another journey.

The Book

Nathan does indeed become Gerald's PA. But more than that, he becomes his co-author.

After a decade without publishing, Gerald feels the need to address the next generation of Christian men on the issues of sex: sex before marriage, self-gratification and porn. Pornography and the Christian man is, as far is Gerald is concerned, the big unspoken issue of the century within the church. If he needed proof, Nathan is it. With free porn readily available on the internet, Christian usage is at an all-time high, and discussion of it is almost non-existent.

Porn is addictive. Soft porn leads to hard porn. This can lead to deviant behaviour. And all of it a no-go area for the average church conversation. Or the average church preaching for that matter.

Gerald and Nathan work hard on the book, with Nathan's own dramatic story in the first chapter. *Sexual Healing* is published in early 2013 and the roadshow begins. Gerald and Nathan are everywhere. The tour is aimed at men, and within a short time more than thirty churches in different locations have signed up to host them.

One of the first is Portsmouth. They put out a press release to the local newspaper announcing 'Porn Sunday'. This is picked up by the *Sun*, then *The Times*. A week or two later, the BBC are on the phone. Can Gerald speak on the Jeremy Vine show?

A phone interview follows. Radio Four take an interest. There are more interviews. Then it's Nicky Campbell on Radio 5 Live:

'The problem is, Nicky, people in the church are not being honest about it. Most young men wank. But it's not something that gets talked about.'

Yes, you read that correctly.

Gerald quite often uses the 'W' word.

'Well,' says Nicky, 'let's keep it clean shall we, let's keep it clean!

Shall we be a little more Christian with our language?'

Gerald argues that it's the language of young people. It's the way he has to speak if he's to get through to them. If the price of reaching a generation caught in the trap of pornography is the use of the 'W' word, it's a price worth paying. If he doesn't address these issues, who will?

'Pornography is the battle of the Christian church in the twenty-first century,' says Gerald. 'It's availability on the internet and its use by young Christian men, with the resultant guilt and shame, could wipe out a whole generation of potential Christian leaders! We have to address it!'

There are many who agree. Rachel Gardner is founder of the Romance Academy, and another person Gerald has invested in. She describes Gerald as 'punching the darkness' with his uncompromising stance on the subject of sex:

'While others keep quiet, Gerald speaks out.'

20

FATHER AND FRIEND

Three boys. Each very different. Today, one is a Director of Housing for the YMCA, another a landscape gardener (Gerald and Anona have an amazing back garden as proof) and the third a successful financial trader in the City of London. Each has picked up different traits from their parents. The caring, the creative, the networking.

It's all there with Gerald and Anona. The compassion is obvious when you talk to them. Years of ministry, the experience that goes with the pain and loss of Pioneer People. But most of all the passion to continue, to serve, to seek God for all He has for them.

At 70-plus, Gerald has no thoughts of retiring. And if he has begun to think of it, it seems God has other ideas! At a recent conference, Paul Weston, one of the leaders in Pioneer, comes over to Gerald. He invites Gerald to stand. As he looks at him, Paul speaks a prophetic word:

'Greater are the latter days than the former days! It's your vision that's paved the way for others to walk on and through. You and Anona saw the vision years before others even glimpsed it. It's why you're a pioneer. And the best is yet to come for you both, but also for the Church, the bride you have given yourself to for most of your life.'

Not everything Gerald does is on the main stage. Ever the prophet and pastor, the two are reflected in one of his most important – and often unrecorded – roles as a father and friend to the next generation.

There's history here. One of Gerald's main regrets with regard to his own family is that he didn't have a close relationship with his dad. There are reasons for this. It's partly the more formal society of the 1950s, and partly the crisis moment when Gerald appears to have stumbled on the fact his dad may have had a mistress.

Whatever the reason, it's something that has made Gerald doubly aware that he needs to be on the lookout for young men who need a father's helping hand. Pastoring people is a gift of Gerald's anyway. Add to that a deliberate mentoring of young men he prophetically sees are on the verge of finding their own life-calling, and you see one of Gerald's hidden and very effective ministries.

Again, God has prophetically spoken into this. In 2009 Gerald becomes increasingly aware that there needs to be a new generation of young men and women moving into leadership. He feels compelled to help, but he's not sure how it will be seen – an older man mentoring much younger men. He needn't have worried. At a conference in Sheffield, Ben Woolard, one of the main student leaders at Sheffield University, points to Gerald and says that God has a word for him:

'You will be a father and you will jump a generation. You will spend a lot of time with young adults – this will be misunderstood – but you must do it!'

A Christian Guy

It's a cold spring morning in 2005. There's a blackbird doing his best to announce the new season has arrived. Two men are sitting on a park bench in Parliament Square. The sun is winning and the early chill has gone. No chill in the conversation either. It's intense. The young man is called Christian. Christian Guy. Yes, really.

Christian has had a long-term calling to work in parliament. As he speaks with Gerald, so many things become clearer. The theology is challenging. The motivation to know God's direction, uncompromising. The thinking, unconventional. Gerald is due at another meeting. He cancels it to continue the conversation.

Later, Christian is a passenger in Gerald's RAV4 (the number plate it came with is L44CAR; Gerald says this is L for Leatherhead, 44 the year he was born, and CAR – well, you've got that bit). Another lovely day. Gerald is playing Elton John's *Made in England* CD at quite a high volume. It is a wonderful moment. And a confirming one. This is the man Christian wants to serve and spend time with. He wants to learn from Gerald and begin his adventure towards the call God has on his own life. Christian moves in next door to Gerald and Anona with some friends, committing to a time of working with Gerald, being mentored and encouraged. Then back to the dream of working in Parliament.

Until recently, Christian headed up the think-tank Centre for Social Justice, with an increasing influence upon Parliament and on the nation. At the time of writing, Prime Minister David Cameron recently appointed Christian Special Adviser to Downing Street on Welfare Reform and Opportunity.

Christian recalls that conversation in Parliament Square as being the defining point that led him to the calling he has today.

Not long ago Gerald was invited to the National Prayer Breakfast at the House of Commons. As Gerald arrived, he left his coat with the attendant and said, 'I'm looking for a Christian Guy.'

The lady looked quizzically at him.

'Well, as I understand it, this is a Christian prayer breakfast,' she replied, pointing into the room. 'There's plenty of them there. Take your pick.'

Prophetic Encounters

Whole lives have been shaped by Gerald's prophetic encounters. The musician Noel Richards is an obvious early example, as is Steve Clifford, long-term friend and fellow leader, today running the Evangelical Alliance.

It's Gerald's ability to see God at work in unexpected places that often results in changed lives and an impact on the community well beyond the expected.

Another meeting. Another city. Ministry time at the end. Gerald is moving powerfully, bringing a number of prophetic words and words of knowledge to different people. He points to one man, then another, a lady here, one of the leaders over there. Each with a word from God, delivered by Gerald from the microphone.

Gerald turns. In front of him is a 14-year-old boy.

'And you, young man, need a Father. God is going to bring a Father into your life.'

The meeting moves on. The boy doesn't.

At the end, he comes over to Gerald.

'Please. Will you be my father?'

Gerald doesn't know what to do. 'Oh, Lord, I've stepped over the mark this time, haven't I?' he whispers in prayer.

'Tell me about your father.'

'I don't have one. He walked out when I was a year old.'

'Is your mother here?'

'Yes, she's at the back.'

Gerald reckons this will solve it. The mother will explain to the young man, whose name is Luke, that it's not that easy to adopt a father, and clearly Gerald isn't the man. This meeting is in the south-west of the country. Gerald lives in the south-east. Too many miles. No relationship. The obvious thing to do is to pray for the right father.

At least, that's what Gerald thinks the mother, Penny, will say. She doesn't.

'This is what I've been praying for all of Luke's life,' she says. 'This is God answering prayer!'

A couple of days later, Gerald is on the phone to Penny, discussing what this is supposed to mean in practice. Surely it's just too impractical?

'Not at all,' says Penny. Luke will come to stay for a week or two each year. The idea is just to fit in with Gerald's timetable.

He arrives for the first time complete with a scrapbook, to show Gerald and Anona his earlier life and where he lives. There's a picture of him outside his mum's flat. The road is Coates Road.

Luke visits regularly, but eventually Penny finds a new man. Gerald thinks this will change the relationship.

'I'm so pleased for you, Luke. You've got a new dad.'

'Yes, but don't you see?'

'What do you mean?'

'Gerald. Mum's got a new man in her life. She doesn't need me so much now. I can come and live with you!'

Despite the relationship not working out for Penny, circumstances allow Luke to live with Gerald and Anona for a while. Luke stays in the church for several years after that. He's now married with children and helps lead a church in the Wirral.

Other Sons

Gerald's in the States, speaking at a conference. Church leader Tom Hare is there, with his son Thomas. Over a meal Thomas asks Gerald:

'You didn't see me at the conference, did you, Gerald?'

'No, I don't think so.'

'I was there. And I felt God speak to me about you.'

Well, thinks Gerald, *this is a turn up for the books – someone with a word for me!*

'God says you are a father. I'm coming to England to go to college. Will you be my father?'

Another one. Thomas does indeed stay with Gerald and Anona.

James

Not the States this time, but Chichester. Gerald is in a coffee shop. Early for a meeting, he's sipping his latte. Gerald can't get the young man who is serving the coffee off his mind. He feels God is saying his name is James. And Gerald has a word for him.

Leaving his coffee to cool, Gerald goes out of the coffee shop to buy a card, writes it back at the table, puts the name James on the front and gives it to the young man.

Yes, he is called James. More than that, he is living with local church leaders Roger and Maggie Ellis. The chances of that being a coincidence? The population of Chichester is around 24,000. A probability of 24,000 to 1. God's kind of coincidence. And another son blessed.

Dan

Gerald is being interviewed on Premier Radio. It's there that Bob hears him. Bob is a Methodist care worker and he plans to bring the boys he cares for to one of the church meetings in Leatherhead.

Gerald sees Dan (name changed) in the congregation. He feels God has something to say to the young man, so at the end of the meeting he asks for some time with him and Bob. Dan, effectively born a drug addict and subjected to childhood abuse, gets prayed for. But God has a bit more than that planned for this particular young man.

It turns out that Dan is only temporarily with Bob and his wife and is in need of a home. Gerald and Anona pray. There's no lack of people in and around their home but they sense God is prompting this link and they agree to take Dan on.

The first problem after moving in is to sort out the charges against Dan. He's due in court for burglary, aggressive behaviour and other misdemeanours. Gerald goes with Dan to the court hearing.

The judge is rather officious.

'Who is the gentleman next to the defendant?' he asks.

Gerald is allowed to speak and explains that he and Anona have taken Dan in, and are now helping him to change his lifestyle.
The Judge doesn't know what to say. Something of a first there, no doubt. He is astounded that anyone would act in such a sacrificial way towards a juvenile defendant.

'Young man, I'm not going to give you a custodial sentence. It seems to me that you are in a place where you can be helped and supported. I hope you realise what an opportunity this is! I've not seen this before. Don't waste the chance.'

Dan doesn't. His life changes rapidly. Free from drugs and alcohol, he finds faith in God, gets baptised in water and is soon joining Gerald on different missions.

The Seizure

Sadly, it doesn't last.

Months later Gerald is called home from a meeting one Friday night. Dan is out of control. He's drunk. Aggressive. Abusive. And by the time Gerald arrives home, Dan has been taken away by the police.

The next morning Gerald wakes up to find he can't move. Just a turn of the head. That's it. Unable to move his limbs, unable to twist his body. Anona's already up and about downstairs in the kitchen.

Gerald shouts for help and asks for a doctor.

Eventually, some ability to move returns and Gerald is able to shuffle down the stairs and await the doctor's verdict. He's worried it's some kind of stroke.

It's not. It's stress. Tension spasms. This most unflappable of people is stressed. Not by the big meetings or the VIPs he meets, but by a boy named Dan, whom he loves as a son and feels he has somehow failed.

As Gerald recovers that day, he recalls an early prophecy over his life. It was brought by the charismatic church pioneer from the States, Jean Darnall. In it she says that people will see Gerald appearing to leap from mountain-top to mountain-top. But most will have no idea of the valleys in between he has to walk through. And God's assurance is that He will be with him in the valleys. Before climbing the stairs to bed that night – something of a literal valley to mountain-top moment for Gerald as he struggles with the seizure – there's a prayer on Gerald's lips:

'Thank you, Lord. Thank you that You are with me in the valleys as well as on the mountain-tops. Today is a valley. It feels deep. It feels dark. But I give you this moment, just as I give You Dan. Touch his life again, Lord. Bring him back.'

Not every story has a happy ending. As this is written, Dan is still without a living faith in God and is struggling with his addictions. But he has met the Lord. And God has a way of calling back His prodigals.

Gerald and Anona have what Gerald calls a 'battle theology'. On that basis, they continue to pray, refusing to give up. One day . . .

The Girl at the Back

She's at the back of a meeting on a Sunday evening.

During that meeting, Anona feels compelled to go to the front and speak through the microphone. This is a rare thing for her.

'There's someone here. Everyone thinks you're a Christian, but you know you're not. And tonight's the night to sort that out. Please come and talk to me afterwards.'

That, you would think, was that. But it's not. Remarkably, Anona feels she should say it again. So she goes up to the microphone for the second time.

'There's someone here. Everyone thinks you're a Christian, but you know you're not. And tonight's the night to sort that out. Please come and talk to me afterwards.'

People are looking at her with some concern. Why the repeat session at the microphone? Has Anona somehow forgotten she has just spoken? But that's not all. Again, Anona feels God impressing on her that she needs to repeat the invitation.

So, for a third time Anona picks up the microphone and repeats the same words. This is embarrassing. People are really beginning to wonder.

Anona spots the girl at the back. It's more than that. It's as if God has highlighted her. Anona knows this is the girl she went through the embarrassment for. After the meeting, she goes over and asks her if she's the one.

'Yes', says the girl, 'yes, it's me.'

Anona leads her to a new faith in God. Anona's persistence and willingness to look foolish helps the girl find faith that night.

Move on a few years. Pete Greig, leader of the 24/7 prayer movement, comes to stay with his wife, Sammy. Gerald asks them how they found faith in Christ. Sammy says, 'Well, you know that!'

'Not sure I do?' says Gerald.

'Well, you don't come out of it very well, Gerald. But Anona does.'

It turns out that Sammy had originally attended a larger

meeting at Tolworth where Gerald was the speaker. Sammy had gone forward at the end of the meeting to pick up some literature and everyone thought she had responded to Gerald's message. But it's on a second church visit that she does respond. The girl at the back. Anona's persistence.

A Face in the Crowd

Gerald is a guest at a big Christian event at the NEC in Birmingham. Near the end of the worship time, Gerald takes a look around from his seat near the edge of the stage. There's a man. Second row back, third on the left, in one of the VIP seats. Gerald senses it so clearly – a transforming word from God. But how to reach him? Well, as always, if this is from God, He'll find a way!

Fast forward to a coffee break between meetings.

'Gerald, I'd like to introduce you.'

And there, in front of him is the same man he saw standing in the meeting.

'I wonder,' says Gerald, 'I wonder whether we can find somewhere to talk?'

Gerald and his companion take the man to one side.

'God was telling me in the meeting about you. He wants to deal with some stuff in your life that is holding you back. When you were young, you were abused, weren't you?'

The man nods quietly. A tear falls. He's a young musician from Nashville, and is seeking God's direction for his ministry.

'You have worn shame on your shoulders like a cloak,' says Gerald, 'but God is lifting the cloak from you, taking away the shame and the trauma.'

As Gerald and his friend pray for him, the man senses a supernatural touch of God through the Holy Spirit.

The young man wrote to Gerald recently:

'Your prophetic ministry was the turning point in my deliverance from the shame of childhood trauma. The words, "You have worn shame on your shoulders" will be forever etched on my spirit as the words of Jesus, just for me. Those words put me on the ultimate course towards complete freedom.'

Facebook Friends

Gerald has a lot of Facebook friends. Nearly 5,000 of them, in fact. The maximum number allowed. Gerald has to 'drop' friends to accept the requests of new ones.

He uses Facebook as a platform to let people know of his Christian activities as well as to write some thought provoking and provocative statements – everything from sex before marriage through to the Muslim radicals and a Christian response. Why do it?

'Sometimes you feel you are a lone voice talking about these things,' says Gerald, 'but I'm not fussed about that. When you begin to speak out, others quickly come out in support who would otherwise stay silent.'

It's while on Facebook that Gerald is asked for a new 'friendship'. His name is Chris and he's out in California. Chris explains that his father has often spoken of Gerald and has his books. Fair enough. The Facebook link is made.

It's two years later. Gerald has posted something on Facebook. He sees Chris has viewed it and made a comment. As it's to do with English church history, Gerald is a bit puzzled. A young man in the States interested in UK Christian history is a little unusual. There's something about Chris. As he looks at the Facebook picture, Gerald feels prompted to contact him.

A phone call later, Chris has explained that he's not American, but from Bolton. He and his twin brother are out at Bill Johnson's church, Bethel Church, in Redding, California, completing a two-year study course.

Gerald gives some of his background and in view of the church history post Chris had been looking at, mentions Leatherhead is the last place John Wesley preached before he died.

'Well that's interesting,' says Chris.

'Why's that?'

'Some guy here in Bethel Church prophesied over me and my twin and said we have the spirit of John and Charles Wesley on us. To be honest, we'd never heard of the Wesleys at that stage. So we've made a study of them over the last two years.'

The twins are about to return to the UK at the end of their time in California. Gerald invites them to stay in touch.

Once they are home, Chris phones. He feels a prompt to visit, and the twins duly arrive.

It's not long before Chris is convinced he's meant to stay, but is not sure what to do about it.

Back to Bolton. Gerald is up there, speaking at a meeting. He arranges to meet Chris and Jack on the Sunday morning after the conference.

And it's an excited Chris and Jack that he meets. It turns out that they were at a different prophetic conference the day before. An Australian speaker pointed to the two of them. She said to Jack, 'God is calling you as an evangelist.' And then to the two of them, 'In fact, the spirit of John and Charles Wesley is on you both!'

The twins hit the floor at that stage, under the power of the Holy Spirit. As did their father, who had been looking on.

And all this comes out on that next Sunday morning in Bolton as they speak with Gerald. It's clear that they also feel Leatherhead is where they should go. The last place John Wesley spoke. The first place for them to begin their ministry.

That same week, a local school contacts Gerald and asks if there is any help Gerald can offer in terms of Christian support and assemblies. Enter Chris and Jack, 20-year-old twins with a passion for Jesus. Along with Gerald's youth worker, Rachel, they regularly work in the school. The headmaster sees what is happening and asks for help at another school as well. And then some finances arrive.

Just the start.

Seventy

As this book goes to print, the head count is over seventy. Seventy plus young men have directly asked Gerald for help, primarily in the area of pornography. Recalling the prophetic word over his life to 'jump a generation' in his mentoring and discipleship, Gerald continues to speak into the darkest areas of Christian life, often neglected or deliberately avoided by many a Christian leader.

21

HOPE

Gerald is being driven through Cobham by an influential local lady. He wants to impress her, to tell her how a life can be changed. As they are driving, they approach a man on a bike.

'Take that man,' says Gerald. 'His name is Norm. Until recently he was a useless loud-mouthed individual with big problems. God has completely changed him!'

Just at that point, the lady drives a little too near to the cyclist. The cyclist shouts back, performs a 'v' sign and uses a number of expletives. If you'd seen at Gerald at that point, there would have been a slightly red face. He's still prone to the odd exaggeration.

No Hope

Or how about the time Gerald is driving along through a village and sees a car beginning to roll backwards. He sees the driver is walking to the post box, but he's obviously left his handbrake off. Gerald leaps out of his own car, runs across the road and pulls up the handbrake of the runaway car.

There's a guy behind him who has just pulled up as well, gesticulating wildly.

'What does he want?' Gerald asks himself.

It's then he sees where the man is pointing. Gerald's own car is now rolling rapidly down the hill. Gerald has done exactly what the other driver did! No hope.

The quote from A.W. Tozer seems rather appropriate: 'Save me from myself and from all the injuries I may do myself while trying to be a blessing to others.'

Another time, Gerald is in the States and at a meal with a number of American pastors. They don't drink alcohol. It's not the done thing in a lot of US church cultures. But Gerald wants a glass of wine.

He's teased about it incessantly, to the point that Gerald shouts out 'Oh Jesus! Help me with these wretched Americans! What I would do for a glass of wine!'

The wine waiter arrives in an instant.

'You called me sir? What would you like?'

He's Hispanic. Gerald looks up at his name tag: 'Jesus'.

Sometimes others decide to give Gerald no hope. Like the time he was seen carrying a whisky crate into his chalet at a Spring Harvest conference. It cost him an invitation to a church. If only the person had asked – it was full of books and sound equipment!

New Hope

But there is hope. Real hope. And in Gerald and Anona's later years, it's showing itself in abundance: in lives changed, in books written, in messages preached. And in a new way in Leatherhead.

It's Martin Smith, the songwriter and musician, who writes to Gerald and Anona after the decline and fall of Pioneer People. 'Gerald, it's time to tend your own garden again.'

A time to stay at home and to build again. Today, Pioneer Engage is a flourishing new Café Church in Leatherhead. The congregation is growing. A new generation is coming on line to lead. Well-known guest speakers such as former politician Jonathan Aitken and evangelist Jonathan Conrathe are regular speakers. And Gerald and Anona are in their element.

In 2015 a number of evangelism initiatives have been started, supported by Jonathan Conrathe. In one week more than 600 people are reached. Many are prayed for, and with a team of twelve on the streets each day, there are a number of salvations and recommitments to Christ. At the end of the week, a fun-day mixed with worship and healing completes a successful week for this dynamic new church.

Gerald quotes the business guru Peter Drucker: 'The best way to predict the future is to create it.'

He is.

Hope for Uganda

Gerald has travelled the world. For the most part this has been preaching in churches and conferences. Press Gerald and he may be able to remember a few of these trips, but it's all a bit of a blur. What isn't a blur though, is the trip to Uganda.

The Archbishop of York's brother is in Uganda. He has read of Gerald's work with AIDS sufferers, so a meeting in Uganda is arranged.

After this meeting there's an all-night prayer meeting. And straight from there, Gerald is taken to the home of the Minister of Security in Kampala.

There are soldiers outside with guns. Gerald is greeted by the Minister.

'So, Mr Coates. When do you think Jesus is coming back?'

Not sure what to say, Gerald remembers a quote from Tony Campolo.

'Sir, I'm not on the programming committee, I'm on the welcoming committee.'

It breaks the ice. There is much laughter and many helpful discussions. As the party begin to leave, Gerald hangs back, pretending to look at some books. He has something to say to the Minister.

Gerald has had a vision during his meeting, of the Minister's house completely surrounded by hostile troops. Gerald explains. The Minister takes it seriously. All the security is tightened, not just for the Minister of Security, but for the Prime Minister and many of the other cabinet ministers in government, and 2,000 troops are placed around the home of the President.

Within a short space of time, homes of some of the cabinet ministers are attacked. The government troops are ready for them. Hope for a nation.

. . . And ongoing prophetic words for a nation. Whilst in Uganda, Gerald meets a smartly dressed man. He stands out from the crowd by his demeanour as much as by his suit.

'Sir, I think the Lord would be pleased were you to run for President of this country.'

The young man smiles.

Today, he is governor of the Gulu district of Uganda, which includes the town Gulu and over three hundred villages. He has regular meetings with the current President and his cabinet.

Hope for Ministry

Gerald has been a particular encouragement for the disgraced UK cabinet minister Jonathan Aitken. Jailed for perjury, and finding a Christian faith in prison, Jonathan is an occasional guest at Gerald and Anona's. The funny thing is the people that drive him there. Most are ex-cons. Big, burly men you wouldn't want to mess with are Jonathan's new friends, many of them gloriously saved from their past.

Jonathan Aitken remembers that first meeting with Gerald,

years before. He was at a low point: on the verge of a prison sentence, with his wife divorcing him. He knew he needed help. At that first meeting at Marsham Street, Gerald prayed for him. Jonathan liked the man. He saw a genuine care – someone who could help. A prayer partnership began.

Gerald is there after prison too. He's there at their home the day Jonathan and his daughters face the bailiffs following bankruptcy – as a result of the the court case that led to perjury. And Gerald is there the day all the young people in church lay hands on Jonathan and pray for his future. Jonathan sees this as a key moment in terms of God's blessing on his life and the new life he now lives.

Gerald encourages other ministries. It's something he does. Always on the lookout for a word of encouragement or a prophetic word, many have seen their own ministries grow as a result.

Steve Chalke is given a microphone badge prophetically by Gerald, long before he becomes a regular face in the media.

The famous pianist Bobby Chen has benefitted from many an evening with Gerald and Anona, his legal guardians, while he was at music school and away from home.

Christian cook Graham Kerr and diet and fitness pioneer Rosemary Conley have visited in the past. Anona is careful not to cook for these particular guests!

Speaking Out

Gerald is not afraid to speak out, of course. The comedienne Joan Rivers said, 'I succeeded by saying what everyone else is thinking.' That's pretty true for Gerald too. We think it. He says it.

Take the atheist Richard Dawkins's 'There probably isn't a God' campaign, where the Dawkins slogan went up on the side of buses: *'There's probably no God. Now stop worrying and enjoy your life'*.

'I for one welcomed the campaign,' says Gerald. 'The more

money Dawkins spent on those posters, the more it led to discussions about the Christian faith.'

Gerald helps lead a counter-campaign 'There probably *is* a God': *'There probably is a God. Now stop worrying and start looking for him. He is everywhere.'*

'In the world of Richard Dawkins's atheists,' says Gerald, 'there is no YMCA/YWCA, no Christian Aid, Tear Fund, Christian youth organisations, Christian faith schools, or the continual funding of Christian charities by churches around the world. No Christian architecture reflected by the cathedrals, abbeys or cloisters in our nation. Hardly any Classic FM – dependent as it is on music relating to Christ's birth, life and ministry and biblical events.'

He may not be an original thinker, but Gerald's willingness to speak out ensures debate. And the gospel is heard as a result.

One funny anecdote from the Dawkins campaign: Richard Dawkins uses a couple of child models in his advertisements. Alongside a picture of the children is the phrase *'Let these children think for themselves.'* Actually they do! They are the children of a couple in a Pioneer church!

Big Numbers

Gerald has continued to speak at large conferences and influence many in their faith through his challenging words. He's not letting age or, to be frank, a bit of excess weight stop him from speaking, preaching and prophesying. He has been recorded by United Christian Broadcasters, telling his story to many. Add up the dates in Gerald's diary and he's speaking on approximately ninety days in 2015.

He preached in Mexico, with the musician Jarrod Cooper helping at the meetings. Crowds of 13,000 and more filled the 10,000-seater building. To this day, Gerald thinks it must be a reverse multiplying miracle that got them all in! More importantly, as Jarrod sang his well-known song 'King of Kings' in Spanish each night, the hundreds who came forward to commit their lives to Christ were an inspiration to keep going.

Gerald has particularly fond memories of preaching at New Song Christian Fellowship in Nashville, USA. There is such a presence of the Holy Spirit at every meeting, above and beyond what Gerald has been used to. He sensed an empowering in his preaching. There was such an anointing on the meeting that no one who attended could fail to be affected by it. Word got out. And one of Gerald's friends called to ask what was going on. It was reported in the Christian media and reported in the papers. Many travelled to be there.

Big numbers and small numbers.

Stepping Down

It's 2007 and Gerald knows it's time to step down from running the Pioneer Network. He's been leading the Pioneer Network of churches since its beginning in the mid-1980s. There needs to be a new leader. But who?

Talks begin with some of Gerald's closest friends and advisers. They agree. But they are no nearer knowing who it should be.

It's early evening in a London restaurant. Gerald is there with some of his Pioneer leaders. They have had guests that day – Billy and Caroline Kennedy. Billy and Caroline lead a network of churches from their centre in Southampton and have been working with Gerald's leaders with some change management workshops over eighteen months or so.

Talk turns to Gerald's successor. There's a joke about Billy and Caroline being there. Caroline is giggling.

'What's the joke, Caroline?'

'Oh it's nothing. Just coming up in the car I had this absurd thought – what if Gerald handed over Pioneer to us! So funny!'

Everyone laughs. Except Gerald.

Gerald can't think straight. There, in the restaurant, God is giving him the way forward. He doesn't know Billy and Caroline all that well. He respects them as leaders, he's appreciated their help – but to take over Pioneer? Surely it has to be an insider who knows the history, has more of the DNA? There has been no discussion relating to this.

Move on to another leaders' meeting. Steve Clifford chairs it. Should Pioneer continue? If so, who should lead? Everyone speaks. None are willing to raise the issue that Gerald should step down. Finally Steve asks Gerald what he would like to see. Gerald recounts the successes over the years. The losses too. He confirms his commitment, but . . .

'I don't see me leading. I'm happy to stay for a while but I need to step down. And I think Billy and Caroline should take it on.'

There is relief at first that the network will stay together. And then amazement at the recommended choice.

But a few months later, the joke is a reality. The Pioneer leaders accept the change. There is an excitement. It is all so obvious now. How had they not seen it?

Today, Pioneer is continuing to grow. Under new leadership, it has added further churches and has reached well beyond its new church boundaries to work with many denominational churches. It is becoming a network of apostolic networks. The network is bringing new life into the Methodist movement, sharing as it does a similar Wesleyan theology and passion for social engagement.

Billy is well aware of the privilege of leading this movement and of its legacy: 'The new church songs. The open worship. The influence and impact it has had on mainstream church life. The whole idea of groups in the home. There's so much more . . . And we're still pioneering!'

Beginnings and Endings

Bryan Price, Gerald's childhood friend, has been off the scene for many years. Gerald has lost touch, although he knows he lives in the Salisbury area. Gerald and Anona are down there one day for a meeting. There's time to spare, so there's a walk around the town centre for Gerald while Anona shops. And there is Bryan! Sitting down in the town square.

It's a wonderful time of catching up on life. Together with Anona and Bryan's wife Jennifer, they have lunch together, reminisce together.

A few months later, Bryan dies of a mystery illness. Psalm 139 talks of God writing down every day of our lives. We don't know what the next moment will bring, but He does. And that includes special moments such as the meeting of Bryan and Gerald before Bryan's death. God's plans include unexpected moments. And for Gerald, a special moment of rekindling a long-lost friendship. Something to be treasured.

Recent years have included other unexpected moments. In particular, a number of reconciliations of relationships from the past. None more so than that as a result of the phone call from Bryn Jones.

There had been little or no contact between Gerald and Bryn since the parting of ways of their respective church groupings in the late 1970s, although both had made a number of attempts at reconciliation as late as the mid-1980s. But towards the end of his life, beset by health problems and too ill to manage all the teaching himself, Bryn invited other leaders in to help teach his next-generation leaders. Gerald was one of those invited. It was timely, and brought about a fuller reconciliation between Gerald and Bryn.

Hope for Leatherhead

Carl is a pastor from the South West of England. He's relaxing near the end of a long day. He looks up. In front of him, in the room, is an angel. The angel speaks.

'My name is Hope and I live in Leatherhead. Leatherhead has come to the attention of the Lord. As Wesley preached his last sermon there, so again, the Lord's name will be known.'

Carl is a friend of Gerald, but not so close as to know the Wesley connection, nor to know the history of John Wesley. He calls Gerald and tells him, 'There is hope for Leatherhead.'

And that isn't the end of the story. As Carl and his wife prepare for bed that evening, suddenly there is a shriek.

'Carl! Carl! There's an angel in our bedroom!'

Carl's wife has no idea of what happened earlier on that evening. But there in front of her is an angel.

When God wants to underline his purposes, He does so emphatically!

Prophetic words from angels are not the only words for Leatherhead. Sharon Stone, a teacher with a prophetic ministry, had spoken years earlier of Leatherhead again being a place of strategy for the nation. Gerald hadn't been too sure of the word at the time, but some investigations had identified that Winston Churchill had used a house in Leatherhead in the Second World War, as a base for many of his key meetings with officials. So, from Churchill's strategy for the nation to God's strategy for the nation.

Who knows how all this will work its way out? One thing is for sure. God hasn't forgotten His purposes for Leatherhead. Or His purposes for Gerald.

Royalty

It's hard being a leader. Harder still when you feel called to bring a difficult message.

Prophets have an ability to get into trouble – just read the Bible!

There is no doubt that the battles over the years have taken their toll on Gerald. He speaks of a new generation taking over from where he is leaving off. A generation without the scars of battle, but with the same vision and understanding of God's kingdom. He's aware that some of the emotional scars make it difficult for him to continue with the same energy as in earlier years.

One of the most common comments about Gerald is that you can either love him or hate him – but it's hard to ignore him! Perhaps that's the way God sees it too. He certainly hasn't ignored Gerald. In the hardest of times, there have been key prophetic words for Gerald and Anona that have encouraged them and kept them on track with all that God has for them.

As Gerald moves into his seventies, these prophetic words continue. And not just the directional ones. Sometimes it's just good to hear how God sees us.

Another conference and a lady approaches Gerald.

'Excuse me, I don't know you, but do you have anything to do with royalty?'

Gerald pauses. Reflecting on his links with the Romanian royal family, he replies, 'Yes, I do.'

'Well, look after yourself because God sees you as His royalty.'

'From This Day Forward'

In a field, at a boy's camp, a young Gerald has prayed a prayer. 'From this day forward, please make out of me what you want me to be.' God takes Gerald at his word. And that is the story you have just read.

It's quite a story.

'If you're unsure what to put on my gravestone,' says Gerald, 'put "We, by God's grace, changed the heart and face of the church in the UK."'

Bold words. Some would say arrogant words. It seems Gerald is keen to ensure he's controversial all the way to his grave!

But history shows our churches *are* different today because of the house church pioneers that have gone before us. A whole church movement was born. House churches. The March for Jesus. Worship groups. Scripture in song. Open worship. Hands raised. Bible weeks. Marching in the streets. Football stadiums filled with worshippers. The influence on parliament and on royalty. The influence on the established church. The prophetic. The apostolic. The Baptism in the Spirit. Words of knowledge. Team leadership. And a kingdom message sounding to the world. Much that was lost to the church back in the 1960s is with us today; we have a God of restoration.

The whole reason for this book is to record, rejoice and respond. To record the story. To rejoice – to say 'thank you' to God for being able to live in the good of that story. And to respond with our own lives as part of that same story.

As Gerald says in one of his sermons, 'We have a choice. We can be voyeurs or participators. We can look at history or we can affect history. It's our choice.'

From a few young people in the front room of Tartar Road, to a worldwide influence.

There is much God still has in store for a youthful seventy-something prophetic leader called Gerald Coates. From this day forward . . .

ENDPIECE

It's a Tuesday afternoon and Gerald is approaching the doors of Number 10 Downing Street, the guest of the Prime Minister. He thinks to himself: *Somehow. Somehow we have to reach these politicians.*

Late in the afternoon two days later, after a day of book writing. Gerald has been talking for most of the day. He does talk a lot. It's said that the leaders at Pioneer restrict him to just one story per meeting! There are notes everywhere and a good deal recorded onto a laptop as well.

As the laptop is turned off, Gerald looks out of his lounge window. There's a group of school kids passing by.

'Somehow,' says Gerald. 'Somehow, we have to reach those kids.' Whatever you think of this man, whether he fits with your theology or not, whether he inspires or annoys you, one thing is for sure. He's as passionate today as he was all those years ago when those first friends began to gather in his front room.

From a pioneering house church leader, through to pastor, prophet and movement leader, the passion is the same.

Gerald's is a story worth knowing, a story worth reading. What many enjoy in churches throughout the UK today is as a result of Gerald and his fellow pioneers. As hundreds of thousands gather this Sunday in charismatic and Pentecostal churches up and down the country, they may not know it, but what they have – much of the teaching, the worship, the freedom in the prophetic – can be traced back to pioneers such as Gerald.

Mistakes? Yes. But so much more. Lives changed. A whole nation affected. From the kids on the street, to Number 10.

The laptop is packed away. The pages stacked.

'Oh,' says Gerald, 'just one more thing . . .'

Endpiece After the Endpiece

By Gerald Coates

Yes – but there really is one more thing! I didn't realise that Ralph would try to be funny, but then he didn't know that the publisher would ask me to make a response to his writings.

So – one more thing!

Firstly, thanks for reading this book. It may be that to some I seem to have gone from mountain-top to mountain-top. But Ralph was keen that the valleys of loss, betrayal, and sometimes personal failure were also featured. Such is life. He was right.

Success is the ability to survive failure!

I want to record how grateful and proud we are of our sons: Paul, his wife Lisa, and their children Lola and Ava; Simon, his wife Ekpen and son Ethan (and a new brother/sister on the way); and Jonathan, hardworking and on the lookout for a wife! They have added so much to our own marriage. I recall one Christmas when there was so much laughter at the dining table that I had to leave the room and sit in the lounge – I was in so much pain simply laughing.

So now to Anona: little of my story would have been possible without her love, skills, pastoral concern and patience. Her ability to run a complicated household, with a growing family, my office, staff team, regular callers, and my frequent absences, quite often at times when we had little money, is amazing. This book is a credit to her faith and commitment to Christ and His people.

I should also record those who opened significant doors and provided platforms for me, some recorded in this book and others not already mentioned. Clive Calver and Peter Meadows, Spring Harvest; Roger and Faith Forster, Ichthus/Revive/MFJ; Barney Coombs, Basingstoke Baptist Church/Salt and Light; Dave Tomlinson, Festival; Stuart Bell, Grapevine/One/Ground Level Network; Mike Pusey, Farnborough Baptist Church; Don Double, Good News Crusade; Danny Smith, Jubilee Campaign; Alan Kirbey, Monkton Combe School; Andrew Owen, Destiny; Stuart Brunton, The Gate; Sandy Millar, HTB/Focus; John Coles, New Wine.

And further afield: Ernesto Alonso, Mexico; Dale Evrist, New Song Christian Fellowship, Nashville; Ché Ahn, Pasadena; Peter Lyne and the Garrett family, both New Zealand; Robert Kayanja, Uganda; Helen Lock and Pastor James, Uganda; John Arnott, Toronto; Rudi and Billa Pinke, Frankfurt; Max Schlapfer, Switzerland; John Hartley, Nashville; Tom Hare, Cleveland; and the late and dearly loved Norman Miller, UK/Nashville USA.

And this book, if written at all, would have told a different story were it not for friends and advisors: Noel and Trisha Richards, Dr Mica Jazz, Roger and Margaret Ellis, Peter and Sammy Greig, Lynn and Marti Green, Graham Kendrick, Dave and Pat Bilbrough, Paul and Amanda Williams, Jenny Moore, Gary and Joyce Jenkins, Carl and Mel Wills, and the already mentioned John and Christine Noble, Steve and Ann Clifford, plus the new Pioneer leaders Billy and Caroline Kennedy and Paul and Paula Weston. All of these have played various but important roles, but it would be remiss of me if I did not record my thanks. There are others of course, names lost in the mist of time, and others who have moved on or moved away.

One of the hardest things for me, and no doubt Ralph, has been squeezing seventy years of life, relationships, work and ministry, into a few chapters. You may be disappointed that your name was not featured, and maybe felt you deserved at least a word! You probably did. But it should be remembered I did not write this book, it was written for me and about me, and I turned Ralph down twice before Anona convinced me I'd made a wrong decision. He is the one who has decided what to include and, as an objective observer, important people sadly must be left out of the story. This is a book – not a library! Even as we were about to go to print, my mechanic, Ray, pointed out that at the beginning of my ministry he drove me around various parts of the UK. Thank you Ray.

And finally, to Ralph. What can I say? I never planned on a biography, and were it not for Anona there would not be one. Ralph was keen to be accurate, fair, when necessary critical, and give credit when due. I love the style, pace, and occasional quip at my expense. All of the stories you have read were in the public domain, many within a small circle. But anything shared with me over the last few decades of a confidential nature, from the highest in the land to young guys struggling with porn, has remained in my heart and prayers – they are not for this book.

The challenge, at whatever age you are, is to pioneer and never settle. Whether in circles small or large, you will experience that there is a world of difference between following models and having to be the model. As with important people Ralph or I have left out of this story, it is true that much of what we go through, particularly the valleys, is known only to a few. But the Great Bookkeeper has recorded it all. Books of the living and the dead, the Book of Life, your name, sacrifices, patience, tears, and hard work when carrying on can seem so difficult, is all to be rewarded. Just imagine, being rewarded for what we should have done in the first place, if we hadn't messed up! What a God, and what a Saviour.

Most of us seek pleasure sometimes to avoid pain; others of us appear to press on for no apparent reason, even with laughter and joy.

Whatever our personal future and that of our world, we can live by something we cannot see.

Those who dance are thought mad by those who don't hear the music.
Attributed to Friedrich Nietzsche (atheist!)

So keep listening and keep dancing!

Oh – one more thing! Thanks Harry for the haircut (I promised him that). Front cover.

About the Author

Ralph Turner is a leader and director of KingsGate churches and is part of their Leicester congregation. He is married to Roh with four adult children. Ralph has worked in the pensions industry for most of his career. He is an author and blogger.

You can find more at www.mountain50.blogspot.com